Dying to Live Abundantly!

Living in the Love, Joy, and Peace of the Lord

at 40, 50, 60, 70, 80, 90 and 100+

DR. ROBERT ABARNO

R
E
S
CRUCIFIXION U
R
R
E
C
T
O
N

To my Professor Dr. Wilson with Thanks RA

Soli Deo Gloria!

To GOD ALONE
BE THE GLORY!

I am the resurrection and the life. He who believes in Me, though he may die, he shall live. And whoever lives and believes in Me, shall never die. Do you believe this?

JOHN 11:25-26

Scripture quotations, unless otherwise noted, are from the Holy Bible, New International Version (North American Edition) ©1973, 1978, 1984 by the International Bible Society, Zondervan Bible Publications.

Scripture quotations marked NKJV are from the New King James Version. ©1979, 1980, 1982, 1983, l985, 1990.

Scripture quotations marked TLB are from The Living Bible. ©1971, Tyndale House Publishers Inc., Wheaton, Il 60189

Library of Congress Cataloging in Publication Data

Abarno, Robert

DYING TO LIVE ABUNDANTLY!
Living in the Love, Joy, and Peace of the Lord at
40, 50, 60, 70, 80, 90, and 100+

232.9
Library of Congress Catalog Card Number 95-94086

ISBN 0-9631575-1-5   Softcover

DYING TO LIVE ABUNDANTLY!
LIVING IN THE LOVE, JOY, AND PEACE OF THE LORD
AT 40, 50, 60, 70, 80, 90, AND 100+

Table of Contents

Biblical Truth is Reality

This book is designed to debunk humanist presuppositions about aging, dying and death which have environmentally affected Christians and non-Christians alike. Jesus debunked these malignant presuppositions as the eternal Living Word...

> *For God so loved the world that He gave His only begotten Son that whosoever believes in Him should not perish but have eternal life.*
>
> *JOHN 3:16*

As a Christian counselor/psychologist I have worked for more than twenty years with thousands of patients. It grieves me when I hear the negative mindset expressed about aging by a youth-driven, contemporary secular society. Movies and the print, radio, and TV media have negatively impacted a significant group of 40+ people with regard to aging. What is deliberately suppressed by the media is the positive living experiences of Christ-centered 40+ men and women. One of Satan's vehement denials is that by faith in Jesus Christ many people are living in the love, joy and peace of the Lord with enthusiasm. The benefits of aging in Jesus is a well-kept secret!

Instead of the 40+ years being a blessing, the aged have become a burden to themselves, their families, and society. Conversely, the Bible gives us countless examples of men and women who never feared aging and therefore lived productively in their latter years. Consider Abraham and Sarah, who were 100 and 90, respectively, when Isaac was born. After their son's birth Abraham and Sarah continued to serve the Lord. Once God demonstrated His power to use them, Abraham, Sarah, Moses, Caleb, Anna, the Apostle John, and others had biblical intimacy with God and therefore enjoyed His purpose for their lives at 85+.

God Himself is ageless. This fact alone should set the tone for all people about aging. The Bible states that in Jesus we will enjoy the eternal presence of our ageless God (John 3:16). Why fear aging if God has promised to give us abundant life here and now and for all eternity? (John 10:10b). Sadly for those who are aging in despair, this is one of Satan's attempts to destroy our faith in Jesus. The despair involved in aging implies that aging is a curse rather than the blessing God intended the wonderful years of aging to be. Despair about aging is a lie of Satan which continues to immobilize a large segment of the Christian population. These Christians are beguiled by Satan and kept from fulfilling their mandate from God—to live abundantly and thereby publish the good news (Ps. 96) of the love, joy and peace of the Lord.

Abundant life in Jesus Christ can dispel the false assumption that aging is the worst time of life. My prayer for this book is to convey to the reader that biblical truth in the form of biblical intimacy with God is long lived reality. My prayer for the readers is that by faith they will know what God has in store for those who love Him (1 Cor. 2:9). As we age, our lives in Jesus become a

Love, joy, and peace in Jesus is truly God's biblical healing prescription for aging.

blessed and holy paradigm of His love and grace. At 76, I have just begun to discover what God has in store for me. Writing this book is a joyful, exciting part of that discovery process. Love, joy, and peace in Jesus is truly God's biblical healing prescription for aging.

> *When someone becomes a Christian he becomes a brand new person inside. He is not the same anymore. A new life has begun!*
>
> 2 CORINTHIANS 5:17 TLB

Remember, in Jesus Christ older is not better...it is best! We like God become ageless. Don't let Satan keep your abundant life in Jesus a secret! Let your life be a living

Remember, in Jesus Christ older is not better...it is best!.

love letter from God to a sick and dying world. Live your life here, now, and for eternity in the fullness of God's love, joy and peace. A new life for eternity has begun! Let His will be done.

Dying to Live Abundantly

Aging and living here and now abundantly (John 10:10b) is something I have pondered since I was 40 years old. As I began to age, the pleasures of life seemed to be more fleeting with each passing year of my life. I prayed for insight about aging. The Lord revealed to me that I must die to self to live abundantly. I now rejoice without fear that aging in Jesus is living abundantly for eternity. The love, joy, and peace of the Lord are the reality of my life. How did all this come about?

The Holy Spirit revealed to me through scripture the meaning of a biblical truth I had heard many times. God, the infinitely wise Creator, made us in His image and likeness—yet each of us different from one another.

> *I have been led by the Holy Spirit to share with others that "being in Jesus" is better than "doing in the world."*

God said whatever He created, including you and me, is very good (Gen. 1:31). By His grace (Eph. 2:8-10), I enthusiastically agree! My being is in Jesus. I have been led by the Holy Spirit to share with others that "being in Jesus" is better than "doing in the world." My being in Him is essential to doing His will in my life here and now and for eternity. Praise God!

I am different from everyone else. God's purpose for my life was decided by Him before the beginning of time (Psalm 139, Eph. 1:3-12). In His infinite wisdom God designed each person according to His plan. My model for following God's plan is Jesus. He is the Lord of my life, therefore, I am Christ-Centered![1]. Now I am learning by following Jesus to come out of the wilderness of dying and death into the promised land of life in Him,

---

[1] Christ-Centered Personality Development, Dr. Robert Abarno, ©1988. Second Edition 1992, Third Edition 1994, Fourth Edition 1996. All rights reserved.

here and now and for eternity.

Very slowly, millimeter by millimeter, I am engaged in a two-stage self-discovery process. Stage One of this process is crucifixion. The only crucifixion I have ever thought about is the crucifixion Jesus endured for my sins. The Holy Spirit has led me to understand that aging is crucifixion, the death of my physical body. I am actually dying in my physical body day by day. Yet in Jesus there is abundant life—not fear—because He is my eternal provision. As I age I am comforted by the Holy Spirit to embrace crucifixion.

Few of us think of, speak, write about, or dwell on aging as a type of bodily crucifixion. Death in the form of crucifixion is frightening and painful, and we don't want to think about our own death. We'd do anything to avoid aging and death. I am at peace. I have been able to reconcile my crucifixion—my death—because Jesus promised in His Word that I will enjoy abundant life in Him now and forever.

Simultaneous with my aging process is God's continuing plan for my life. That plan didn't end when I turned 40. In Stage Two of the self-discovery process, my soul is regenerated—resurrected. As my soul (mind, will, and emotions) abandons itself to God it is transformed by His Spirit (Rom. 12:1,2) into a Christ-Centered personality[2] (Gal. 4:19), and I reflect the image and likeness of Jesus (Gen. 1:26-27).

People fail to understand that in Jesus, dying to live abundantly is aging to perfection in His love and watchcare.

Lazarus' resurrection is a model for me. Just as the burial shrouds were unwrapped from Lazarus' body as he emerged from the tomb, so are the superficial pressures and concerns of life stripped away from my soul as I move closer to the Lord (John 17:3). When Jesus becomes our focus, real love, joy, and peace come into our lives, and at 40+ we are "resurrected" to a new life in Christ without fear of aging.

---

2 Ibid.

This two-stage process of crucifixion of self and resurrection of the soul continues as we learn to live abundantly through a more intimate knowledge of Christ and His plan for us.

People fail to understand that in Jesus, dying to live abundantly is aging to perfection in His love and watchcare. The love, joy, and peace (Gal. 5:22,23) are taking place in me here and now. As I age in Jesus I am being resurrected by God. What is there to fear about aging and death? I embrace my crucifixion and my resurrection, which is reality with Christ.

My soul/personality (mind, will, and emotions)—my uniqueness as God has created me to be—will live forever in the resurrected body God has prepared for me.

> That is why we never give up. Though our bodies are dying, our inner strength in the Lord is growing every day. These troubles and sufferings are, after all, quite small and won't last very long. Yet this short time of distress will result in God's riches blessing upon us forever and ever.
>
> 2 CORINTHIANS 4:16-17 TLB

Then my eternal soul, my uniqueness, will inhabit my eternal heavenly body in the love, joy, and peace of the presence of Jesus:

> ...when we die and leave these bodies—we will have wonderful new bodies in heaven, homes that will be ours forevermore, made for us by God Himself, and not by human hands. How weary we grow of our present bodies. That is why we look forward eagerly to the day when we shall have heavenly bodies which we shall put on like new clothes. For we shall not be merely spirits without bodies. These earthly bodies make us groan and sigh, but we wouldn't like to think of dying and having no bodies at all. We want to slip into our new bodies so that these dying bodies will, as it were, be swallowed up by everlasting life. This is what God has prepared for us and, as a guarantee, He has given us His Holy Spirit.
>
> 2 CORINTHIANS 5:1-5 TLB

Being Resurrected Here and Now in the Love, Joy and Peace of the Lord

In the Foreword I comment on crucifixion and resurrection. Resurrection begins with salvation. By salvation and the infilling of God's Holy Spirit resurrection begins here and now, and continues throughout eternity (John 3:16). During my research for this book, God by His grace has enabled me to experience Christian biblical resurrection.

In this book I indicate that resurrection is a process beginning at salvation, imputed and imparted to Christians. Vine's Expository Dictionary[1] renders the word resurrection in the Greek as "**anastasis, exanastasis, egersis, egeiro.**" I have added a few notes (italics mine), to share my experience in Christian biblical resurrection.

"**anastasis**–by metonymy (substitution) of Christ as the Author of resurrection"[1] (John 11:25). *I have also described resurrection, in* Christ-Centered Personality Development[2] *as the ongoing process of sanctification...while we Christians are still alive and present in this world.*

"**exanastasis**–the out-resurrection from among the dead".[1] *Exegesis reveals that biblical resurrection means; I am living here and now among the spiritually dead. My resurrection at my salvation is "from" or "out of" this evil world to life in Christ. My resurrection is ongoing despite being alive in this humanistic world of* **virtual reality**. *By God's grace I experience* **exanastasis**, *as the out-resurrection from among the dead.*[1] *My resurrection is reality in Christ*

---

1 Vine's Expository Dictionary, Thomas Nelson Publishers, Nashville, TN., 1985.
2 Christ-Centered Personality Development, Dr. Robert Abarno, ©Fourth Edition 1996.

here, now, and for eternity. "In order that I may attain to the resurrection from the dead" (Phil. 3:10-21) for His glory.

"**egersis**–a rousing, (akin to **egeiro**, to arouse, to raise) is used of the resurrection of Christ."[1] In Matt. 27:53 resurrection took place, "coming out of the tombs."[1] In 1 Peter 2:9 *Christians are described as* "a royal priesthood, a holy nation a people for God's own possession, that we do proclaim the excellence of Him who has called us out." **Exanastasis**; *from among the walking dead of this world.* "After His resurrection they entered the holy city and appeared unto many"[1] (Matt. 27:53). *1 Peter 2:9 is the purpose of the Christian biblical experience of resurrection.*

My resurrection is reality in Christ.

We, who are in the "process of sanctification" (Gal. 5:22-25), are resurrected here on earth, in this world, to be like Jesus. As we age beautifully in the Lord we become living witnesses of His love, joy and peace.

Heaven is our home. Today, here and now in this world Christians are to live resurrected lives (2 Cor. 5:17) among the sons and daughters of this humanistic world (the walking dead). Having our being in Christ Jesus we know[2]:

Where we come from.

Who we are.

Why we are here.

Where we are going.

We are strangers (out of sync) in this humanistic world, yet we rejoice with Jesus that we are His resurrected witnesses of sacrificial love and grace (John 15:12). Enjoy!

---

[1] Vine's Expository Dictionary, Thomas Nelson Publishers, Nashville, TN., 1985.

AGING

The Triumph of Christianity Over Humanism

For since by man came death, by Man also came the resurrection of the dead. For as in Adam all die, even so in Christ shall all be made alive.

1 CORINTHIANS 15:21-22

The view of aging shared in this book shows the triumph of Christianity over humanism. If I were my own god, I would grow old without responsibility or accountability but with great fear, constantly asking myself the questions, "Why do I have to die? What will happen to me when I die?" In English-speaking countries almost everyone has heard about Jesus Christ and the fact that He died so that we can have eternal life (John 3:16), yet many people still reject these claims. Many humanists rationalize that unless you die you will not take on another life form (i.e. reincarnation).

If I were my own humanist god, I would not have a problem with sin despite the biblical fact that the wages of sin is

The world is in despair. Humanism is a world rooted in the ego/sin nature of pantheistic Greek thought which has over the centuries eventuated into hopelessness.

death. Humanists live for the immediate moment—the here and now. If they step out of the immediate moment, then they have to face the thought of death. To avoid facing the reality of aging and dying they must have constant distractions (i.e. entertainment or alcohol and other addictions) so that they do not have to think of what will happen to them when they die. Their philosophy and world view is immediate gratification. They engage in idol worship and lose the potential for the good that God intended for each person He created.

Humanists' idols are philosophy and science, which are the basis for the religion of humanism. With "aids" from society, humanism has been adopted as the world standard for the quality of human life. Why then does the question persist...is life fulfilling and secure or is life simply existence? Why are AIDS, abortions, drug addictions, and crime on the increase? Why is suicide on the rise among our young people?

The world is in despair. Humanism is a world rooted in the ego/sin nature of pantheistic Greek thought which has over centuries of time eventuated into hopelessness. Socrates, Aristotle, Plato, and other Greek thinkers established the foundation for humanism by presenting the concept to the world that each man or woman is his or her own god. Later, Aquinas in his Summa Theologica, with misguided theological license, tragically linked humanism with religious tradition. Humanism when presented under the guise of religion, fails to focus on whether man or woman is god over his or her own life, sin, dying and death.

> *In Christ, the problem of my death because of original sin is resolved.*

Biblical truth which has withstood the test of time records original sin and rejects the notion of man or woman being their own god. Unlike the humanist who will not acknowledge individual sin, I cannot deny the fact that I sin. However, in Jesus Christ I can repent, confess my sin and will be forgiven (1 John 1:9). The humanist refuses to consider the claims of Christ because each humanist acts as his/her own god and therefore is in effect, sinless. The humanist as his/her own god cannot acknowledge sin, but without success denies the reality of death and dying.

In Christ, the problem of my death because of original sin is resolved. However, for those outside of Jesus Christ, the problem of death remains. Impending death in the form of aging is a constant nagging, conscious threat that never goes away. The more humanists see, read, and hear about the death of prominent people, the more they fear their own aging and subsequent death. A humanist will not engage in a conversation about aging, dying and death.

> *Eternal peace does not exist for humanists. This does not have to be the case. Jesus is not exclusionary.*

The humanist, without any answers regarding dying and death, ages with prideful fear and anger as constant companions. The humanists' use of denial, avoidance, rationalization, and other defense mechanisms does not provide them with peace. Therefore, the secular humanist has no control over their future, which inevitably includes aging, dying and eternal death. Eternal peace, the love and grace of the Prince of Peace does not exist for humanists. This does not have to be the case. Jesus is not exclusionary (John 3:16). The humanist is self aborted from Jesus without hope in this present time or for the future. Denial of aging, dying, and death is also denial of eternal life in the love, joy and peace of the Lord beginning here and now.

Conversely at 76, my life in Christ is more like a daily awakening than a preparation for death. The relaxing wisdom of faith tells me my life has only just begun. To die does not mean the transient nature of death, it means new life for eternity with Jesus. I believe the truth of the Gospel with all of my being, and peace within my soul (mind, will, and emotions) prevails!

In this book, I write about biblical relevance, God's gift to those in Jesus at 40, 50, 60, 70, 80, 90, and 100 years of age. God has blessed me with a life of biblical relevance. My spirit joins God's Holy Spirit, and I soar. As my spirit soars, my whole being is energized to confront in love the foreboding humanistic philosophy of hopelessness related to aging, dying, and death.

Christ is ageless, so in Him I am ageless. Rather than spend time and energy in the humanistic mode of dying daily with pride, fear, and anger, Jesus commanded us to "occupy until I come" (Luke 19:13b). Will you join me in dying to self in this hopeless humanistic world? **Will you become vibrant, alive, here and now and for all eternity, in the love, joy, and peace of the Lord?**

Christ is ageless, so in Him I am ageless.

If You Talk the Talk, Then Walk the Walk

Application and accountability are essential to avoid using age as an excuse for not being all you can be for Jesus, yourself, and others (Matt. 22:37-39). Daily application of my faith motivates me to live in the love, joy, and peace of the Lord. I am not preoccupied with dying and death but with living here and now and for all eternity.

My accountability is to Jesus. It is my joy to be accountable in obedience to Him, to walk like Jesus and thereby fulfill the Great Commission (Matt. 28:19,20; Acts 1:8). I also rejoice in being accountable to love others as Jesus has loved me—sacrificially (John 15:12).

> *As committed Christians age beautifully in the love, joy, and peace of the Lord, "His way, His truth, His life" (John 14:6) becomes our talk and our walk!*

Finally, as I apply my biblical faith under the guidance and direction of the Holy Spirit in obedience to His Word, I become His person here in this world. If I am His glory as He declared (John 17:10), then I am here and now and for eternity, a manifestation—a mirror image of Jesus (Gen. 1:26,27)—in the coming Kingdom of God here on earth (Matt. 6:9,10).

As committed Christians age beautifully in the love, joy, and peace of the Lord, "His way, His truth, His life" (John 14:6) becomes our talk and our walk! Jesus in His prayer to His Father God blesses us beyond measure when He prayed for us:

> *I in them and You in Me, all being perfected into One—so that the world will know You sent Me and will understand that You love them as much as You love Me.*
>
> JOHN 17:23 TLB

Introduction

This book addresses:

Who am I?
Why am I here?
Where am I going?

Throughout our life here on earth there is an underlying uneasiness about what happens as we approach the end of life as we know it. The Bible makes abundantly clear what God has in store for us eternally—everlasting life. (John 3:16).

At 76, the Lord Jesus by His grace and mercy has given me some insight into my own aging process. Instead of being sad and lonely I have experienced a love, joy, and peace which I attempt to share in this book. There is reality to aging which of course I did not experience in my younger life. I missed many things earlier on in life because I did not understand the reality **of my being in Jesus,** i.e., **who am I?**

My life is full and exciting! I live expectantly each day as I experience in Jesus a self-discovery process which opens up a whole new world of possibilities! Many of these possibilities have now become reality, much to my amazement, i.e., **Why am I here?**

Jesus is the difference between the walking dead and those who are undeniable alive and well in Him.

The infinite complexity and sophistication of a person as created by God is beyond description. I have never met a person who has even begun to approach the potential God has built into them (not withstanding the many beautiful, intelligent, charming, loving, generous, kind people I have met in my 76 years). Scripture tell us:

*...no mere man has ever seen, heard, or even imagined
what wonderful things God has prepared for those who
love the Lord.*

1 CORINTHIANS 2:9 TLB

For those readers who do not know Jesus as personal
Savior and Lord, I lovingly suggest you stop wasting time and
your life. Jesus is the difference between the walking dead and
those who are undeniably alive and well in Him. Jesus is the
abundant lifegiver here and now and for eternity (2 Cor. 5:17
TLB).

For those who are in despair about aging, this book may
be a "wake-up" call to give up retirement in body, soul, and spirit. God is not retired! God is ageless! Become fully alive in Jesus
and see what He has in store for you!

Who I am, why I am here (the purpose of my life), and
where I am going is being revealed to me daily by Jesus
through His Holy Spirit.
This self discovery process
I enjoy as a gift from God.

*Who I am, why I am here,
and where I am going is being
revealed to me daily by Jesus
through His Holy Spirit.*

Can you handle Jesus'
plan for your life (Eph. 1:3-
12)? You are part of His
plan of abundant life (John 10:10b). Can you with joy envision
the fullness of eternal life that begins when you place your trust
in Him? Watch with excitement what He has in store for those
who love Him! Take it from one who is constantly surprised by
the love, joy, and peace of the Lord.

*You have let me experience the joys of life and the
exquisite pleasures of your own eternal presence.*

PSALM 16:11 TLB

Dying to Live Abundantly

Writers have lives similar to other people. To put this book into a realistic perspective I begin with a personal experience that may help to explain the title.

On a beautiful Saturday in late October 1996 as I was jogging with Dr. Yancey Culton at the Duke University track I felt a dull aching pain in the upper quadrant of the left side of my chest. We had completed eight quarter mile laps. Our usual Saturday AM routine was twelve laps and then a "cool down" of one more lap.

I felt uncomfortable with this pain but not anxious or fearful. I slowed down and began to walk. I told Yancey that I was getting tired. He knows my age (76) and my level of energy. We walked one more lap. The dull aching pain persisted. As we climbed the fifty stadium steps up from the track to the parking lot I crossed back and forth between the aisles to help delay the straight up climb to the top of the stadium.

I did not share my pain with Dr. Culton preferring to attribute the pain to pleurisy or some chest/lung infection. As we drove back to Yancey's house the pain ceased.

From October of 1996 to March 15, 1997, I continued to experience this dull aching pain whenever I exercised. During that time frame the pain had moved from my chest to the upper left quadrant of my back. The change in location of the pain reinforced my theory of chest/lung infection. I never considered that chronic pain in my back had anything to do with my heart.

Nevertheless, the pain pattern persisted during exercise. I would walk about six minutes then a dull aching pain in my back would begin. Pain would continue, forcing me to slow down. After four to six minutes of pain, the pain would gradually abate. The remaining fifteen minutes I would walk at a normal pace without pain. Therefore, I was reinforced in my wishful thinking despite chronic pain during exercise that my pain was due to some relatively minor problem, or why would it abate? I never considered reference pain which it was, from my heart to my back.

On March 5, 1997, I went to the doctor for my annual (age 77) medical checkup which included a **resting** electrocardiogram. The EKG was unremarkable...no problems were detected. Again I felt reassured.

On March 15, 1997, while walking with Dr. Culton I shared with him the chronic pain I felt while exercising. Dr. Culton's reaction was immediate and profound. He raised hell with me, up one side and down the other. He told me to call my doctor on Monday. He said just to make sure he would also call my doctor on Monday.

Monday, March 17, 1997, I reported in at the doctor's office for a treadmill test. Upon completion of the test, the cardiologist and my doctor were very disturbed. Tuesday, I went to the hospital for a heart catheterization, the results of which further disturbed the physicians. Wednesday, I was in surgery for a quadruple bypass. This surgery, thanks be to God (Soli Deo Gloria) was successful! Then, I was moved to the intensive care unit for twenty-four hours.

My next stop was to a private room on the cardiac care floor. The care I received during my operation and stay in the hospital was superb! I felt as though God had placed me in a five star hotel and I was the star. My wife said that when she first saw me following the operation I was still out, but I looked like anything but a star. I had a tube in my neck, more tubes down my throat and several tubes in my stomach.

Once the surgeon removed the tube in my neck, then later the tubes in my throat and stomach, I felt almost alive. I had not experienced any pain from the surgery, only a numbness in the upper quadrant of my chest and upper left arm. In both of my legs I had long incisions, as well as a long incision from my upper chest down into my stomach area. In addition, there were three one inch incisions across my stomach. Being without pain may have been due to medication, but for whatever reason, I thanked God for His mercy and grace.

I was very appreciative of my wife for her steadfastness, faith and endurance. My son David came to help. He is a Medical Technician in the USAF and took over my care at night in the hospital since my wife had come down with a sinus infection and allergies. The surgeon, staff and Dr. Culton continued to check me out during my hospital stay of six nights and seven days until I was discharged.

While in the hospital I lost my appetite. My weight dropped from 156 pounds to 139 pounds. The sight, smell and taste of food was repulsive to me. However, as compensation my blood pressure dropped from 140/72 to 110/60. My blood sugar went down from 140 average to 112-116. God is so good!

At the doctor's suggestion I enrolled in the Duke University Center for Living cardiac rehabilitation program. This is a medically supervised exercise program that meets three times a week for two hours each session. I also continue to walk with Dr. Culton on Saturday. My strength and endurance are beginning to return. In addition I am able to work every day on a limited basis. I feel alive and well!

I want to thank God and give Him the honor and glory for my recovery by His agape love and grace. Also that God raised up the people who were instrumental in my operation and recovery. God is the Great Physician. I am compelled to share this experience at age 77 to encourage others to look to Christ for resurrection.

It took me four years to write *Dying to Live Abundantly* never thinking I would experience resurrection in this life by God's infinite wisdom. Deliberately my heart was stopped for several hours while my life was sustained by a heart lung machine. God then resurrected me by His love and grace using the skill of the surgical team to resurrect my heart function and my life.

God, in His wisdom, allowed me to experience *Dying to Live Abundantly*. This book consists of life experiences and observations by which I share the love, joy and peace of the Lord Jesus Christ. Nothing that follows is less than it was before my crucifixion and subsequent resurrection. My prayer is that some will relate to the contents of these chapters and positively identify by God's grace with the love, joy and peace of the Lord. Then be moved by His Holy Spirit to share His agape love with others.

CHAPTER 1

My Mother – "The Grand Dame"

A famous medical doctor said, "They have no good answers to old age – nor do I."

Eye has not seen, nor ear heard, nor have entered into the heart of man the things which God has prepared for those who love Him.
1 CORINTHIANS 2:9

But the Godly shall flourish like palm trees, and grow tall as the garden, and are under His personal care. Even in old age they will still produce fruit and be vital and green. This honors the Lord, and exhibits His faithful care. He is my shelter. There is nothing but goodness in Him!
PSALM 92:12-14 TLB

This is a true story of how God continues to work miracles in the lives of people contemporary secular society considers aged and useless. Our culture is driven today by a preoccupation with youth. Yet why are so many of our young people in the "have-it-here-and-now" generation so deeply wounded? Also, why are the Christless 40+ jaded, burned out, empty, walking dead—useless to themselves, their families, and society?

Do you realize that living in the love, joy and peace of the Lord can make our later years the most productive, fulfilling, and exciting time of life? The Bible gives many examples of men and women who have enjoyed their later years with great enthusiasm—Abraham, Sarah, Moses, Joshua, Caleb, Elijah, Daniel, Anna. My own mother's early life was burdensome. Later, actually at 75, she chose to follow the Lord Jesus by dying to self and she began to live abundantly in His love, joy, and peace. Mother continued to be blessed and found purpose and enthusiasm for living for God, herself, and others through the love, joy and peace of the Lord Jesus.

Mother had an elderly friend whose family felt they could not cope with the care that was necessary for her and placed her in a nursing home against her will. Mother was horrified! It impacted her so deeply that she made her four children promise never to put her into a nursing home. For 80 years Mother lived in her own home, caring for herself, and then for the next 15 years she lived with one of her children enjoying relatively good health and independence considering her age.

At 95, Mother fell and broke her hip. She now required constant medical supervision. Sadly, the family decided that there was no alternative but nursing home care.

By God's mercy Mother graciously adjusted to her new environment. She noticed that the staff was under the supervision of physicians and, in her mind, rationalized it was a hospital. Mother did not realize that God had a further plan for her life in the nursing home even at age 95.

As with Abraham, Sarah, Moses, Caleb, Anna, and others, Mother's life in service to God began at an advanced age (Luke 2:36-38). She is a good example that God can use any of us at any age. We become aged to perfection in obedience to His Word and become more malleable for the Master's use.

Mother was 98 years and 10 months of age when she went to be with the Lord. Compared to biblical patriarchs and matriarchs, like Moses who was 80 when he lead God's people out of Egypt, she was relatively young. But she lived out the love, joy, and peace of the Lord at 75, 85, 95 and almost to 100. The most unlikely years of Mother's life were when God used her the most. She had great courage when, at 95, she became actively engaged in service to God where He had placed her, despite her apprehension. She was completely unaware that God had a plan for her later years and had perfectly equipped her for it before time began. For those 3 years and 10 months she was known as the "Grand Dame" of the nursing home.

This is how it all began. As she was wheeled into the nursing home dining room three times a day, she would fold her hands as if she was in prayer. Crowned by a halo of white hair, she looked like an angel. Her appearance was confirmed by her commitment to God to avail herself of every opportunity He gave her. Each time Mother appeared in the halls, at the nursing station, in the activities room, exercise room, or the dining room she had a significant impact on the other residents and the staff. Many of them asked Mother to pray for them.

Mother was cheerful and appreciative with rare exception. I never heard her complain to God about her circumstances. She was a phenomenon in the lives of the other residents and the staff. This is not to imply that she was better than the others, but it was evident to everyone that God was blessing her even at her advanced age. Instead of being totally served by others, Mother was able by God's grace to function productively in service to God. In fact, her age was essential to her role.

Elderly, infirm residents confined in a nursing home and often forgotten by their families long for the love and comfort of a "mother figure" My mother was prepared for this very role when she was 16, and she and her younger siblings lost their mother. She became the mother image to her brothers and sisters. Secondary preparation for her role of "Grand Dame" was the many years she mothered her own four children.

So from 95 to 98+ God utilized Mother as the Grand Dame of the nursing home. Her third experience as "mother" was 79 years following her first initiation. Although the residents in the nursing home were not her children, she felt God had given her the mother role and placed them in her watch care. It was also very interesting that many of the staff came by to see Mother on their rounds during the day. Just to have her look into their eyes, hold their hands, and pray for them was a special comfort they sought from her, and Mother was always available to them. She knew the aloneness most of them felt without anyone to comfort them. Many times in her own life there had

3

been no one available to comfort her. Mother moved among many of these suffering people with the love and compassion of Jesus. Being in Jesus enabled her to do for others despite her age.

Mother meant what she said to each person who came to her. She felt strongly led by God to reach out to the staff. She affirmed the important work they were doing among the residents including herself. She was very appreciative of the care they gave her every day. She was constantly affirmed by the staff and actually functioned as para-staff. Everyone's respect for her was clearly evident.

Mother appeared to be quite capable of relating to each individual in some significant way, particularly with those residents she recognized from the dining room. She also related to three different shifts of staff whom she came to know over the time of her residency. She even ministered as "mother" to the hairdressers, as she listened, prayed for them, and provided encouragement.

She lived out her faith in a depressing environment, but it motivated her to be very productive in her daily life. Mother's personal life was very disciplined; for example, she ate a hearty breakfast, little lunch, and even less dinner. A refreshing hot shower was one of the highlights of her day, and she disliked any delay in taking it. In addition, her personal feminine criteria required a hairdresser appointment on a weekly (no longer than a biweekly) basis. Another important requirement about her personal appearance was her weight. On my three weekly visits I was expected to wheel her to a scale and help her weigh herself. She was concerned that she should continue to maintain her figure. Any gain over 104 lbs. was thoroughly discussed and carefully evaluated.

Exercise was also important! Even at almost 100 years of age Mother insisted on participating in exercise classes to help her avoid the sedentary lifestyle adopted by most residents in a nursing home environment. Although she could walk, her increasing reliance on a wheelchair was added incentive to exercise. She did upper body exercises and leg lifts as well as toss a lightweight ball back and forth to maintain her agility, heart muscle tone, and her coordination. She did not consider any part of her life inconsequential!

Mother had always been active physically. Her father had taught her to exercise daily. Factored into Mother's physical well-being was her need and ability to get ten hours of sleep every night. Once she was tucked into bed, she prayed until she fell asleep and slept peacefully all night, almost without movement. She even had to be awakened for breakfast.

Equally important to her was her daily disciplined spiritual routine. Mother was mentally, emotionally, and spiritually alert and oriented. Her prayer life was vital to her well-being. The most important part of her day was the five to six hours of prayer for her children, grandchildren, great grandchildren, and great, great grandchild as well as the staff and other residents. She regularly informed me how busy she was attending to important prayer requests, prayer for God's protection, and daily direction. God answered many of Mother's prayers. She never failed to spend time thanking Him for His goodness and mercy.

Mother's consciousness of the world was not diminished because she was 98 and resided in a nursing home. Although she was legally blind and could barely distinguish faces, her alert mind and perception increased with voice association. However, the loss of the ability to read her Bible and other books strained her emotional and spiritual resources. By God's grace over time she was able to adjust to the loss of the treasured pastime of reading. God graciously filled in the vacuum with other activities, such as more prayer time and meditation with Jesus.

Few people struggled and endured hardship as she had done in her life and she came out stronger by virtue of those experiences. She survived the loss of two children, four wars, at least three major depressions, plagues, famines, and the destruction of my father's business by fire. She experienced life in many of its tragic forms, but resolution of her faith in Jesus enabled her to be undaunted in facing challenges. Her faith quickened her with a cheerful outgoing zest for life.

Earlier, I mentioned the application of Mother's faith. She gave the staff at the nursing home her love and prayers for all regardless of race, creed, sex, or any form of discrimination. God created all of us equally was the biblical absolute in her relationship with others. The staff and residents knew this. She applied this view to America in general. Her love for the American people and her desire that God prevail required her, in obedience to scripture, to pray for those in authority. Yet she was adamant in her stand against socialism and humanism.

The Triune God; Father, Son, Holy Spirit, and the Bible were the absolutes which ruled Mother's life. Similar to the patriarchs and matriarchs of the Old and New Testaments—Anna, Elizabeth, Mary, the Apostle John, and others—Mother's faith was lived out with graciousness and humility in the love, joy, and peace of her Lord.

Despite a difficult and challenging life, Mother persisted in seeking God. She was 75 when she came to know the Lord. Her life had been very difficult. Early life experiences often prompted her to anxiety, and prior to her decision to accept Jesus as her Lord and Savior, she occasionally expressed fear and timidity. Following her decision for Jesus, my siblings and I were able to perceive a significant increase in strength and peace in Mother's life. This emerged even more in her ministry in the nursing home.

Her faith in Jesus superseded the fear and aloneness she had experienced in her teenage years with great emotional pain. Mother personally experienced a new reformation at 75. Part of her legacy to me in the Lord was the example she became for me and others. I felt led of the Spirit to write this book "Dying to Live Abundantly" to encourage others to use the later years as Mother did with excitement and productivity. Bob Mumford describes this change in Christian's lives at any age, as a "new song" a "new reformation"[1]. Mother experienced a new song, a new reformation at 95, almost analogous to Abraham and Sarah. In her spiritual reformation she was productive and became a mother to more than 150 residents and staff members.

Instead of being "over the hill" at 40+, we can begin a new life for God just as Mother did. He has promised to see our lives fulfilled for His honor and glory. We can enjoy living in the love, joy, and peace of the Lord in this world and are assured of a place in heaven with Jesus. What in Mother's early life prejudiced her from being open to learning more about God sooner?

At 16, after the death of her beloved mother, she faced a challenge—she had to learn to survive on her own. She was born in Ware, Massachusetts, into an Irish-American family. Her maiden name was Marguerite Anna McNally. She said her determination in life was originally attributed to her Irish heritage, but I came to the realization that God in His infinite wisdom and grace had designed Mother for His purpose.

This saint of God began her life in the late 1800's when life was far more arduous than it is now. Under God's watch care and grace, Mother was able to weather the storms of life. Even before her conversion God began to prepare her with determination and energy for life's crises. Only God is able to instill in us what we need in order to follow Him.

Mother's family left Massachusetts and moved to New York City which had a large Irish-American population. My mother and father met there. Both families were Roman Catholic. My father's family were of Italian-American heritage. Both families came to America to seek opportunities denied them in Europe and were delighted with the free enterprise system. They were industrious, hard-working people who over the ensuing years flourished economically and advanced socially. Education played an important role in these processes. Virtue, family values

---

[1] Bob Mumford – Lifechangers, Library Series, Unshared Love, Raleigh, NC, 1995.

and discipline were very important! Crime was non-existent, and indebtedness except to other family members was anathema.

Mother was raised in New York City. Over the years, her father had developed a business as a buyer and auctioneer of antique furniture. He purchased furniture and bric-a-brac from the estates of wealthy people and stored these antiques in his warehouse on Madison Avenue—the same building in which his family resided. The stables for the draft horses that pulled the furniture wagons (circa 1880s) were located on the ground floor of the building. The second floor was occupied by the family. The third floor was home for several individuals who were employed by my grandfather.

Mother's early life in New York was pleasant and fulfilling until the death of her mother. She was very close to her mother who was about 50 when she died. Grandmother McNally had a problem with alcohol which my Mother did not reveal to me until many years later. Although Mother only mentioned it briefly, I observed her sadness and drew the conclusion that Grandmother McNally's death was a huge loss to Mother in terms of protection, security, and companionship. This significant loss left a vacuum in Mother's life which was not filled until Jesus entered her life many years later when she was 75. Mother always spoke of her mother with love, respect and tenderness. Evidently they were very close.

Grandfather McNally was athletic and physically active in his business as well. He continued to conduct business even when his health declined. His weekend regimen when Mother was a young girl was for the family to walk 20 city blocks up Madison Avenue to Central Park. Then Mother and her two brothers and two sisters would jog through the park with their father.

When she was 16, Mother's life changed dramatically—her father remarried. The lady he married had two children of her own. The change in Mother's life became an early 1900s version of Cinderella. Her stepmother had plans for the family which did not include Mother and her siblings. Her father worked hard to develop his business and support his family which now included seven children. Apparently his health failed shortly after his remarriage. Very ill, he was unable to prevent his second wife from ordering my Mother and her siblings to leave their home.

Her aunt took them in temporarily. Mother was sent to a Catholic convent to continue her education, but she did not submit easily to the discipline of the nuns in the convent and soon returned to public school. Later, due to the family's financial burdens, Mother had to leave school and go to work. Because of her aunt's frail health she also had to assume the daily burden of the mother role for her siblings.

One day, discouraged and overwhelmed by responsibility she went alone to sit in a small park. She began to weep. A young boy nearby heard her cry out to God for help. The boy came over and sat down beside Mother and asked her what was wrong. She related to him that she had responsibilities which she could not handle. The little boy suggested she go for help to a Christian Science church in the neighborhood that his mother attended. Until then, she had felt secure with the Catholic discipline she had experienced but, with the loss of her Mother, she did not have the desperately needed intimacy with God. Mother wanted someone to reach out to her in her teenage years who would provide security.

Mother went to the Christian Science church shortly after her encounter with the little boy. She continued in Christian Science for the next 59 years. As a result, my siblings and I were raised in a Christian Science church. Mother was comforted by the kindness and concern of the members of this church who she saw as providing security for her. My Father who was raised Roman Catholic did not attend any church. Although he allowed my Mother to take us to church and Sunday School, he never joined her in this effort.

Mother continued in the Christian Science religion and its

beliefs until she was 75. During the 23 years since my salvation in 1952, I had witnessed to my mother, father, and siblings. I prayed Mother would renounce this cult and turn to Jesus as her Lord and Savior. At 75, in a service in which Dr. Walter Martin taught on the dangers of cults, the Holy Spirit of God claimed Mother for Jesus! What joy I felt that she was finally out of bondage and free as a professing member of the family of God.

During the next 24 years of life that God granted Mother following her salvation experience, she grew in grace and in the personal knowledge of her Lord and Savior Jesus Christ (2Pet.3:18b). Mother had studied the Bible, but now she personally knew the Living Word Jesus Christ. Finally, in Jesus she had the security which she lacked in her life for 75 years. Mother knew something about life and the problems that people encounter in their lives. She knew something about personal loss, being alone, not having anyone with whom to share her burdens. She knew what it had been like to be without Jesus. She was therefore well equipped when Jesus called her to become the "Grand Dame" in the nursing home. She was a devoted Christian lady with long life experience as well as the ability to love and respond to the needs of others (Matt. 28:19,20; Acts 1:8). Mother was strong in the Lord at 95+.

My mother is a wonderful example of dying to self to live abundantly forever.

God used Mother for the next 3 years and 10 months to minister to elderly residents and those on the staff who did not know Jesus. God blessed her with these years of dynamic life which she used wisely for those who He placed in her watch care. For Mother, age was a prerequisite for her ability to minister to others.

I thank God for her life and ministry in Jesus. She is a wonderful example of dying to self to live abundantly forever. Mother knew who she was in Jesus. She had a purpose for her life. She was joyful and productive in service to others in Jesus'

Holy name! She often said "God is ageless and in Jesus I never think about age". Her only goal was a full life in Him. She knew her crucifixion was being completed and that her resurrection was assured. She is now living in the eternal love, joy and peace of the Lord in His Presence.

My Father – Silence until Salvation at 71

My mother loved my father and he in his own unique and unspoken way loved her. While Mother was plagued with fear until her salvation in Jesus, my father never expressed fear or anxiety. Paradoxically, Mother was the one who always assumed responsibility, whereas my father was inclined to avoid responsibility.

After his early retirement at 40, Father was hospitalized with yellow jaundice. His retirement led to a sedentary lifestyle which eventually made him vulnerable to illness. Like many of those outside of Jesus, he resisted living the abundant life. Although I loved my Father, I never really knew him. He was a very private person. Silence would best characterize his demeanor and way of life. His malaise upon retiring was different from my memories of him when we were young children. Then, he was active and involved at home, in family trips, beach outings, golf and swimming.

I have concluded that unless you age in Jesus and die to live abundantly, you have never really lived! The abundance and beauty of aging at 40+ is only experienced in living in the love, joy, and peace of the Lord.

I remember praying for my Father as I continued to witness to him during the last several years of his life. His health was rapidly declining. Two weeks before his death at 71, he confided in me that he was frightened by some of the dreams he was having. He seemed to want me to listen to him even though he had never before permitted me to engage with him at any personal level. I grieved over the many years we had lost through our lack of communication, especially about biblical absolutes that would have enriched our relationship. Although he did not mention his impending death, he knew his time was short.

By God's grace and because my father was in such a weakened condition, he was open and spoke directly to me. I just listened. He said there was no hope for him. Despite this statement I felt led by the Holy Spirit to pray with him even though I had never prayed with him before without my mother being present. In this time of prayer he confessed he was a sinner, repented, and asked God to forgive him. He made his decision to accept Jesus as his Lord and Savior. I rejoiced and gave thanks unto God for His goodness, mercy, love, and grace.

Two weeks later my father awakened my mother at 6 a.m. and asked her to pray for him. The next moment he was with the Lord. My mother telephoned, and I came to their home. I spent time on my knees alone with my Heavenly Father and thanked God for saving my Dad.

Mother had a type of fear which can be intrinsic to people who have been abandoned and cry out to God for security. Father had a type of fear which I can only describe as aloneness, a lack of biblical intimacy with God and family. Before my parents salvation I observed their covert fear of the aging process. There was less communication and more internalization, emptiness, and bare existence instead of the fullness of God's Spirit.

> *In Jesus we have only just begun to enjoy our lives, here and now and for eternity.*

I have concluded that unless you age in Jesus and die to live abundantly, you have never really lived! What I have written and believe is that the abundance and beauty of aging at 40+ is only experienced in living in the love, joy, and peace of the Lord. Jesus is never finished with us. He never abandons or withholds Himself from us. In Jesus we have only just begun to enjoy our lives, here and now and for eternity. This is what happened to my Dad at 71.

> *"When someone becomes a Christian he becomes a brand*
> *new person inside. He is not the same any more. A new*
> *life has begun!"*
>
> 2 CORINTHIANS. 5:17 TLB

Aloneness and fear of aging immobilized my father when he retired from business, family and life at age 40. Without being disrespectful he was among the "walking dead" from 40 until he died at 71. Similarly, many people who are 40, 50, 60, 70+ begin to separate from life. They literally begin to die to family, relationships, productivity and life itself. 40+ people actually age with fear of dying and thus become non-relevant and non-productive for the Lord, themselves and their families. Sadly, this is what happened to my Dad. I am still grieving over the loss of my relationship with my Dad over the last 31 years of his life. Therefore, I suggest you consider the altenative of "Dying to Live Abundantly!" in the Love, Joy, and Peace of the Lord. In Chapter 2, we will examine the stronghold of fear, how it negates productivity, relationships, and disrupts living in victory in Jesus here and now at 40, 50, 60,70+.

My Mother and Father experienced fear as they aged. Does fear of aging affect your life negatively?

❑ Yes   ❑ No

If your answer is yes, describe how?

If your answer is no, describe why not?

Be encouraged! *God did not give us a spirit of fear, but of power, and of love, and of a sound mind.*

2 TIMOTHY 1:7

On a scale of 0–10, rate your level of the fear of aging. ___
Date _____

God knows your innermost thoughts, so be honest with Him and yourself. Do not be filled with the prideful fear of aging.

I trust by God's grace that the reader will understand "Dying to Live Abundantly" is an encouragement as aging is in process. Read on in this book and, as you read, ask God to give you insight into the blessed miracle of aging in Jesus—it's a new adventure!

Aging in Jesus is a self-discovery paradigm! Living in the love, joy, and peace of the Lord Jesus at 40-50-60-70-80-90-100+ has only just begun! Praise God for what He yet has in store for you (John 10:10).

CHAPTER 2

Biblical Relevance – God's Gift to Those in Christ at 40-100+ is Blocked by Prideful Fear of Aging!

arah, Abraham's wife, and my mother had biblical relevance
even in their later years (1Cor.3:18 TLB). They were godly
and remarkable women! God had planned each day of their
lives before the beginning of time for His purpose (Ps.139;
Eph.1:3-12). God enabled Sarah and mother to fulfill His plan for
their lives in productive, exciting, and dynamic ways.

Both experienced the prideful fear of aging before they
fully surrendered their lives to God. They were unaware that
God had prepared and called them for His purposes. Their self-
imposed inadequacy and prideful fear of aging had blocked
them from being biblically relevant. Like Jesus, Sarah and
Mother suffered rejection in their lives. Nevertheless by faith
they learned to experience the love, joy, and peace of the Lord.

Although His grand design for raising up a nation through
Abraham and Sarah was different than the way in which He
used Mother, age in both cases was not a barrier but a prerequisite for effective service. God's infinite wisdom enables Him to
select and use individuals in delightful, if sometimes puzzling
ways to serve Him. God who is ageless is not affected or
impressed by our age. He sees us in reality even at 40 - 100+
as His children.

Sarah knew and proclaimed she was well past child-bear-
ing age and recognized that Abraham was physically unable to
father a child at his age. Similarly, my Mother at 95 reluctantly
agreed to become a resident (a "patient" to use her word) in a
nursing home. Neither age or the prideful fear of aging are any

barrier to God. Despite protestations of age, God worked His plan in the lives of Abraham, Sarah, and Mother with eternal results.

Without purpose for our lives, we decompensate by emotional aging which, in turn, negatively affects our physical stamina. Relevance, our meaning and purpose in life, dies without Jesus Christ. The humanist ages without eternal purpose. Lack of purpose—"Why am I here?"—elicits prideful fear and anger toward God. Anger as one ages is often an outward expression of inner fear of aging and death. Although the humanist does not profess faith in God, someone has to be blamed for the fear experienced during the aging process.

Anger also exacerbates other negative, destructive emotions. People in the aging process find themselves in a state of chronic emotional pain. They are fearful, anxious, and jealous, then react by internalizing intense anger. Confusion reigns supreme, and it is certain that with the impending loss of life anger becomes a significant part of the aging experience. Fear, anger, anxiety, jealousy, and confusion are debilitating emotionally and often lead to depression in those who are 40-100+.

Relevance is extinguished in a flood tide of tears of the 40-100+ fearful, angry person. Alternatively, biblical relevance, the joy of living here and now in the Lord is re-ignited when we are dying to live abundantly for eternity.

It has become increasingly evident with each passing decade of my life that biblical intimacy and relevance are essential for me to live productively for God, myself, and others (Matt. 22:37-39). If I want to know with precision how to measure my life at any age I use the Bible and the Christ-Centered Personality Development[1] tests and measures from my first book. This is a no-nonsense book of practical application and accountability based in biblical reality for every Christian. It contains simple but significant measurements by which each

---

[1]   Christ-Centered Personality Development, Dr. Robert Abarno, ©1988. Second Edition 1992, Third Edition 1994, Fourth Edition 1996. All rights reserved.

Christian can input personal data and easily define their biblical relevance—spiritually, relational, and productively.

The CCPD book asks the basic questions of life which are:

Where did I come from?

Who am I (in Jesus)?

Why am I here (what is the purpose of my life in Jesus)?

Where am I going?

These questions are common to all persons and at some point in life are addressed by each one of us. We search for answers to these significant questions with great longing and passion particularly when we are in a potential stressful circumstance, like aging.

For example, I vividly remember the motion picture "Papillion" in which the main character was imprisoned for years on Devil's Island. Much of his time in prison was in complete isolation. Following one particularly long term of isolation the first question he asked upon his release from solitary confinement was, "How do I look?" His real question was, "Am I still relevant?"

His real question was, "Am I still relevant?"

I was shocked by his appearance. He had aged significantly. His hair and beard were now white instead of brown. His speech was slow and deliberate as he struggled to regain his ability to speak after years of silence in solitary confinement. His pain had intensified due to negative stressful emotions such as fear and anger. He was emotionally driven to know how he was perceived, if only by the prison guard. His guard did not even bother to reply to Papillion's question. Papillion was devastated. He was convinced by this rejection that he was a non-being. He repeated his poignant question, "How do I look?" and again his question was steadfastly ignored by the guard. How sad that Papillion did not realize that God cares! God wants all of us Papillions' to be in the image and likeness of His Son Jesus.

Similarly, in the humanistic world (our contemporary

prison), it is impossible to obtain an accurate assessment of a person's relevancy. We see and hear about love in the world but it is used as a buzz word rather than as the deep agape love of Jesus for whosoever will come to Him (John 3:16).

The Bible is God's love letter to us through Jesus Christ. The Bible is the canon, the measuring rod, the rule of life, the only accurate assessment of human life which is completely honest and trustworthy. The Bible lovingly measures our relevance, by providing answers to the basic questions of life:

Where did I come from?

Who am I?

Why am I here and why now (What is the purpose of my life)?

Where am I going?

The humanist world has no answers to these questions. God's answers are found in the Bible. At 75 I realized that when I was about 40 I began to look for answers to these four questions for my life in Jesus. Since 40 I have begun to understand what God has been teaching me over the years through studying the Bible and by the enlightenment of His Holy Spirit. I am delighted!

However, at age 40+ like Papillion, many of us are tragically arrested in our development. We become prisoners in the solitary confinement of our painful emotions such as prideful fear, anxiety, shame, disgust, revulsion, guilt, jealousy, sadness, sorrow, aloneness, emptiness, and confusion. To further complicate our lives each of these negative emotions include some degree of anger which results in cyclical debilitating pain. We cry out like Papillion seeking answers to the basic questions of life, but the humanistic world has no answers. In fact the world, like Papillions' guard, does not even acknowledge our cry for meaning and purpose.

God has a plan for our lives at 40+ as we commit ourselves with abandon to Jesus Christ the lover of our souls, (mind, will, and emotions). To the question "Who am I?" Christians should respond, as Jesus did, "I AM that I AM". Our biblical response should be, "God is, therefore in Jesus Christ, I am." I have my being and becoming in Him!

Biblical relevance, according to Matt. 22:37-39, states that we should, "love God and love others as much as we love ourselves." God's agape love received and shared with others by me is why I am here. The purpose of my life is the love, joy, and peace of the Lord Jesus Christ.

In order for me to love God I must know who God is.

"God is Spirit, and those who worship Him must worship Him in spirit and truth."

My finite mind is incapable of defining Spirit. Therefore, the Bible also tells me that God the Son was made incarnate. Jesus became flesh and dwelt among us (John 1:14), so in Him I have become biblically relevant. God incarnate in the flesh is Jesus Christ! Now I can clearly understand my being in Jesus is in the image and likeness of God the Son (Gen.1:26,27).

God incarnate in the flesh is Jesus Christ! Now I can clearly understand my being in Jesus is in the image and likeness of God the Son (Gen.1:26,27).

Jesus' purpose for coming to earth in the flesh as the Son of man was to experience all that we experience, such as rejection or abandonment. Jesus was crucified for our sins as a sacrifice acceptable to God so that we might be regenerated by God's Holy Spirit and be acceptable to God. I love God for His plan for my life. I love Jesus for His sacrifice for my life. I am therefore able to love myself as His special creation. I am different and unique from everyone else in my God-created personality, my soul (mind, will, and emotions).

Since I can love myself because God has regenerated me I can love others, too. Jesus said, "I command you to love one another as I have loved you (sacrificially) (John 15:12). I cannot biblically love someone else if I do not love God first. Then because of His agape love for me in Jesus I am commanded to love myself agape in order for me to love others agape. True agape love begins with John 3:16... "for God so loved the world".

My love for God and myself because of Jesus' sacrifice also enables me at 76 to surrender the prideful fear of aging. Otherwise, I will displace on God and significant others my fear of aging, dying and death. Pride and fear are basic painful emotions which negatively affect a person's life. Failure to achieve what selfism (absolutizing self) requires, not what God requires, initiates prideful fear.

Prideful fear then elicits an aura of anger which others perceive immediately because they are threatened by anger. Therefore, as we age we try to prevent ourselves from overtly manifesting anger. We internalize our anger! The emotional cancer of despair is the unwanted consequence of prideful fear and anger.

As a result we are less inclined to be productive for the Lord because of our age. We become immobilized by prideful fear, and anger. These negative painful emotions interfere with godly relationships and therefore preclude us from using our lives productively for the Lord (Matt.28:19-20). We feel like we are out of the loop.

The root cause of aging with despair is pride of life, of becoming old, unattractive, useless which is complicated by the frightening fear of death. We despair as we think that life will proceed without our involvement, without God's plan for our lives being relevant.

Nothing can be further from the truth!

Eye has not seen, nor ear heard, nor have entered into the heart of man the things which God has prepared for those who love Him.

1 CORINTHIANS 2:9 NKJV

*But the Godly shall flourish like palm trees, and grow tall
as the cedars of Lebanon. For they are transported into the
Lord's own garden, and are under His personal care. Even
in old age they will still produce fruit and be vital and
green. This honors the Lord, and exhibits His faithful care.
He is my shelter. There is nothing but goodness in Him!*

PSALM 92:12-14 TLB

Despite these scriptural exhortations about the aging process, we persist in worshipping at the altars of pride, fear, and anger. Therefore, in Jesus' name we should pray that fear can be understood for what it is and not be used by ourselves against ourselves. If we use fear against ourselves we delight Satan who revels in any stressors we generate by ourselves which hamper our faith and practice. These painful stressors disable us from being biblically relevant and productive for God at any age in our lives.

To better understand biblical relevance, God's gift to those in Christ at 40-100+ it would be helpful for the reader to understand the biblical context of pride:

The pride of life, is not of the Father, but is of the world.

1 JOHN 2:16B KJV

Prideful fear and anxiety are often confused with each other. Fear is very specific; i.e., "I am afraid of the neighbor's dog because he will bite me" or "I am afraid of being unable to meet my mother's expectations of me" or "I am afraid of failing a test" or "I am afraid of becoming old and useless without any purpose for my life" i.e., the prideful fear of aging.

There is within me love, joy, and peace as I contemplate God's agape love, mercy, and grace. Consequently I am in a positive sense motivated by "awe" to be like Jesus (Gen.1:26, 27,31). Being like Jesus is awesome and very positive!

Alternatively, anxiety is non-specific, vague, and diffuse, i.e., "I am really uptight and on edge but am not certain what is going on in me. Therefore I am unable to specifically target or identify the problem I am having." Fear and anxiety are both negative emotions. It is important to note that anger is present with both fear and anxiety thus adding to the stress imposed by these painful emotions.

I have been able to identify two specific types of fear. In the positive sense, at 40+, fear may develop in my relationship with the Lord. Fear in relationship to the Lord is positive and may be better described as "awe." This type of fear never elicits anger because it is reverential. There is within me love, joy, and peace as I contemplate God's agape love, mercy, and grace. Consequently I am in a positive sense motivated by "awe" to be like Jesus (Gen.1:26,27,31). Being like Jesus is awesome and very positive!

Fear in the negative sense as we age is always painful, debilitating, and hazardous to our health. Fear sometimes becomes a god who demands constant worship and fear is a sin which can immobilize Christians (1 Pet.5:8). Fear in a Christian gives approbation to Satan and grieves the Holy Spirit.

Because of the painful emotion of fear, we suffer in relationships. As we age we are also susceptible to a retardation of productive activity and service for the Lord.

Fear in the negative sense as we age is always painful, debilitating, and hazardous to our health.

What happens to those who do not trust God? Biblical relevance, God's gift to those in Jesus Christ may be supplanted by stress initiated by prideful fear which is vented as anger. Anger is a painful emotion which is then projected on significant others impairing these important relationships, i.e., with parents, children, husbands, and wives. Any recipient of my anger then responds in anger back to me and elicits from me more fear and anger. This habitual and cyclical process of addiction to painful emotions is destructive of agape love and significant relationships.

Painful emotions are symptomatic of an attempt to have self-dominance over God like Satan i.e., "I will be like God and do it my way!" The ultimate result of deliberate sin in the form of disobedience against God's authority is the loss of significant relationships beginning with God, for which we

> *Finally, the prodigal son realized he was his own problem...He became biblically relevant.*

then blame God (Gen.3:12). Even as we project blame on God, He waits for us with agape love like the father who waited patiently for the prodigal son to return after his selfishness and rebellion. Finally, the prodigal son realized he was his own problem. Then the prodigal son repented, confessed his sin, returned to his father, asked forgiveness, and was restored to fellowship (Luke 15:11-32). He became biblically relevant.

I was asked some years ago to do a consultation where a father rejected his daughter because of his own selfishness. She in turn became angry enough to reject him. Jane came to my office with what she described as depression. She explained that she was a Christian but was increasingly unable to function appropriately. She had been praying that God would help her deal with this painful incapacitating depression.

Jane presented herself as a pleasant, articulate young lady. She was completely unaware of how her father's expectations of her had negatively affected her emotional well-being. She was able to understand that her spiritual life was diminished due to the emotional separation that existed between herself and her father. She concluded that she had miserably failed to meet her father's expectations. Failure in her relationship with her father was in Jane's mind synonymous to failure with God the Father.

Jane had an excellent position in middle management in her company. She took her business career for granted because of her God-given talents and ability. Yet her father never affirmed her significant accomplishments. She assumed she was not successful in her business career because she lacked her father's approval.

Since she was unable to relate to her father, she concluded she would be unable to have a significant relationship with a man. Her apprehension about her father and the fact that she was 40 led her to fear all male relationships. Anger followed fear. Anger at the deepest level of her being was consciously directed toward her father and unconsciously toward God the Father.

Jane was an attractive, articulate, and a pleasant person to work with. She was respected by her peers and well-liked. Yet she avoided opportunities she had to meet single men who expressed an interest in a dating relationship.

Jane became her own problem.

Despite her popularity with her colleagues, the anger caused by her frustration with her father and God was eventually turned inward on herself. Jane was unable to understand that her father's lack of interest and affirmation was not due to her failing him. Her anger initiated other painful negative emotions, and Jane became her own problem. She lost her biblical relevance because of fear.

I suggested to Jane that she was fearful and as a result of fear, a very angry lady. She sat there in utter disbelief. Then she began to consider the possibility that she was angry, and had turned her anger in on herself, thus her depression.

I asked Jane to take time to love herself enough to explore her anger using her bible and a concordance to exegete (draw from scripture) why she was angry. She agreed to do so. We did not set a time limit for this study nor did we set a time to meet again. I concluded from our consults together that Jane would not take much time to work out her anger with the Lord from His Word.

At 9 a.m. the next morning Jane called. She was happy and

excited! She told me she had stayed up until 3 a.m. fascinated with her assignment "to learn to be angry and sin not, and not let the sun go down on her wrath" (Eph.4:25). She asked me if she could come in for a few minutes and share what the Holy Spirit of God had taught her from the Bible about her anger.

She came in later the same day and related that she did not fear God, but out of fear she had made her father her god. Jane also learned that God had created her in His image and likeness (Gen.1:26,27). She concluded therefore that she was not a mistake. In fact, she read and immediately believed "that what God had made was very good" and that included her (Gen. 1:31).

She discovered that in her attempts to please her father she had elevated him above God. Her father's lack of affirmation had bound her in fear as she grew older. She was 40. Previous to this study on anger she had been in despair. Her hidden anger had increased. She had become more withdrawn—constantly preoccupied with what she now recognized as anger. Her colleagues noticed her withdrawal, and she no longer received invitations to socialize. Jane admitted that her work suffered because of her depression. Her ability to function efficiently at work was significantly retarded.

When I challenged Jane to study the Bible about her anger she was virtually hopeless. However, she prayed and asked God to help her by granting her peace and understanding about the problem of anger emanating from fear. The Holy Spirit encouraged her to study.

She began her study by working up a list of things she was angry about. This list provided the basis for searching the scriptures about her anger. Jane came up with 13 computer pages of information from the Bible about anger and other painful emotions which related to her life. She said she was drained from the lack of sleep but jubilant that the Holy Spirit revealed to her through scripture what she needed to know to resolve her depression.

25

We used her biblical discoveries in several subsequent consults to enable Jane to understand her developmental home
environment. The death of her mother as well as her father's
retirement complicated an already depressive environment.
Without his wife and without a job to occupy him, her father's
increasing non-productive, non-relational conduct was perceived by Jane as failure until she searched the scriptures. Her
fathers rejection which was his attempt to control her failed!

Jane was able by the grace of God to answer the basic
questions:

Who am I (in Jesus)?

Why am I here (What is the purpose of my life in Jesus)?

Jane called me six months later and told me with great joy
she was dating a Christian man. Two years after her initial visit I
received a wedding invitation from her. I was unable to attend
because of a long-standing previous commitment but I wrote
Jane and congratulated her on her marriage.

Jane stopped by my office one year later and told me how
she had become biblically relevant in her life by searching out
scripture. We prayed and she thanked God for His love. She
expressed love, joy, and peace about her life. She was not concerned about being 40+ and, in fact, was looking forward with
keen anticipation for what God had in store for her and her
husband in the future.

Jane had many years of service in her job and chose early
retirement to go back and finish college, something she had
been unable to do earlier in her life because of her father's
pressure to get a job. Jane's husband who is seven years older
than Jane caught her enthusiasm about her life and they are
looking forward to their years together at 50-60-70-80-90-100+.

At 40+, biblical relevance quickens the senses with new
awareness and experiences such as listening to early morning
"quiet", then hearing the songs of the birds. To take time to
smell the roses, hum, whistle, and shout for joy are all daily simple pleasures which we can enjoy. Laughing out loud is some-

thing we can enjoy because God loves us. To enjoy the fellow-ship of the saints of like precious faith is healthy. Dying to self-ism is to live abundantly in the love, joy and peace of the Lord.

Being who I am in Jesus in prayer, worship, praise, and adoration are uplifting moments for soul and spirit. All of these delightful pursuits are without cost. Prayer, worship, praise, and adoration stir our blood. We are quickened, and revitalized as we pursue holiness and become His glory (reputation) here on earth (John 17:19,10).

As we become biblically relevant in Jesus at 40+ we can give expression in our Christ-Centered lives by writing books, poetry, music, or engaging in other creative activities free from worldly constraints. As we age we are better equipped with spir-itual insight to see things that are pleasant and of good report which others who are younger are often too busy to observe and enjoy. Living with the love, joy, and peace of the Lord is the healing antidote to prideful fear, anger, and other negative painful emotions.

Enjoy the simple pleasures and blessings that many people take for granted like breathing and the beat of our heart. God enables us as we age to rec-ognize and appreciate these significant and abundant blessings which He provides for us out of His mercy and grace. Dying to self enables one to see the abundance of God's love and grace. Each day I delight and am grateful to God for allowing me to see the full spectrum of colors He provides in flowers, fruit, and

God makes available to us so much quality of life that unless we take time to appreciate and experience His agape love in Jesus we miss the joy and peace of living abundantly in His presence for eternity. Dying without a future is never having lived in the Lord.

vegetables. The colors which God created thrill my heart with their indescribable richness and beauty. My enthusiasm for God is real not manufactured for this book.

About 8 a.m. each morning, the sun strikes a prism on the bevel of a mirror in our bedroom. As a result, the spectrum of colors from the sun are reflected on the bedroom wall. I am unable to give full expression to the depth and beauty of the colors which I inadequately describe here as blue, red, green, yellow, and orange. These colors are so awesome that I do not want them to fade as the sun continues to rise in the east, but remain and be treasured by me and my wife for the rest of the day. The colors last about five minutes. During this special time I stand in wonder at God's magnificent creative power. I am led to pray that God would see my life as a beautiful reflection of the image and likeness of His Holy Son, my Lord and Savior Jesus Christ (Gen.1:26,27).

At 40+ we can enjoy morning prayer when we awaken. We can enjoy vespers time in the evening for prayer, meditation, and thanksgiving to God for the blessings of each day. The minutes before we go to sleep are precious, uninterrupted times to thank God for His watch care over us during the day and throughout the night.

God makes available to us so much quality of life that unless we take time to appreciate and experience His agape love in Jesus we miss the joy and peace of living abundantly in His presence for eternity. Dying without a future is never having lived in the Lord. At 40+ or minus, we can begin to absolutize our biblical relationship with Jesus. Dying to live abundantly in Jesus is an exciting self-discovery paradigm which all Christians can and should experience.

Enjoy biblical relevance:

I have come to give you life abundantly!

JOHN 10:10

It has taken me 76 years to begin to understand how much I don't know about God's agape love for me in Jesus. However, due to God's grace and patience, as I age I am delighted to learn to live more abundantly than ever before. I enjoy each day and look forward to the next day with a keen sense of anticipation in God's love, watch care, and protection.

The prideful fear and anger of aging will disappear to be replaced by an exciting biblical relevance...for all time and eternity in the love, joy, and peace of the Lord Jesus Christ.

Won't you join me in the pursuit of a 40+ awareness of God's grace and love? You will not be plagued by sadness/sorrow because of age. The prideful fear and anger of aging will disappear to be replaced by an exciting biblical relevance...for all time and eternity in the love, joy, and peace of the Lord Jesus Christ.

Am I biblically relevant in my life at 40+?

❏ Yes   ❏ No

If yes, be specific and describe your biblical relevance. Don't be apprehensive. Relax and enjoy what life in Jesus has revealed to you.

If I am not biblically relevant, pray and try to describe why not?

At 40+ am I beginning to divest myself of the world and begin to absolutize my biblical relationship with Jesus?

❏ Yes   ❏ No

If yes, describe specifically how this transition (growing in the grace and in the knowledge of our Lord and Savior Jesus Christ (2Pet.3:18)) is being manifested in my life.

If not, why not?

Perhaps the problems of fear and anger which Jane experienced may be more deeply entrenched than you have realized. Read the next chapter and seek Holy Spirit's enlightenment about your biblical relevance. Remember, God has said, "I will never leave you or forsake you" (Heb.13:5). God has plans for you!

CHAPTER 3

The Problem of Anger Some of the Less Obvious Faces of Anger

W ebster's dictionary defines anger as a "strong feeling excited by a real, or supposed injury often accompanied by a desire to take vengeance or to obtain satisfaction from the offending party. Anger is synonymous with indignation, fury, rage."

The Apostle Paul made four specific references to anger:
1) "Be angry and do not sin, do not let the sun go down on your wrath." (Eph.4:26)
2) "Do not grieve the Holy Spirit of God by whom you were sealed for the day of redemption" (Eph.4:30).
3) "Let all bitterness, wrath, anger, clamor, and evil speaking be put away from you with all malice" Eph.4:31).

Paul wrote the biblical solution to anger which is:
4) "and be kind to one another, tenderhearted, forgiving one another just as God in Christ also forgave you" (Eph.4:32).

Over the years in clinical consultations with patients I have come to understand that anger is an umbrella emotion. Anger is an emotion that is present with other painful emotions such as jealousy, confusion, pride, fear, anxiety, shame, guilt, sadness, sorrow, disgust, revulsion, emptiness, and aloneness. In Chapter 2 and here again in Chapter 3 the correlation of anger with fear is explained.

As a result of prideful fear, reactive anger is destructive to relationships with God, self, and significant others. Anger precludes biblical relevance and Christian maturity. This is especially true of persons over 40 who have kept a record of wrongs, sometimes for years and used them against others as well as themselves.

Anger is a waste of precious time and energy. Fear and anger de-energize our potential for growth in grace and the knowledge of our Lord and Savior Jesus Christ. Alternatively, we are able to enjoy aging (our apprenticeship for heaven) when we are not taken captive by fear and anger which are co-related. In the Bible there are informative personality studies in which prideful fear and anger are acted out even by those who are God's men and women, i.e. Jonah.

The reader may falsely assume that Old and New Testament personalities are not relevant as examples of biblical behavior in our contemporary humanistic society. Nothing could be further from the truth. Many biblical characters encountered the same problems we face, particularly the problem of anger.

At 40+ Jonah was called to go to the city of Ninevah as a witness for God. We read that Jonah disobeyed God primarily because of prideful fear and anger. Although the book of Jonah has been read and taught many times, the principal emphasis is on Jonah being swallowed by a whale. What is seldom recognized is that the book of Jonah has far greater significance than as a children's story. The basic message of this awesome book is Jonah's disobedience to God which caused negative emotions of prideful fear and anger to develop in Jonah's life. Christians should be able to relate to Jonah's disobedience and subsequent painful experiences. Although Jonah did preach to the Ninevites he did so with a reluctant, judgmental, rebellious, and depressed attitude.

In order to properly illustrate fear and anger out of control, we look at the progression of events which finally led Jonah to ask God to take his life (Jonah 4:3). God in the person of Jesus came to give us life abundantly (John 10:10b). We should never attempt to persuade God to take a life He created. God will call us to Himself when He is ready, not because of our fear, anger or despair.

Psalm 139 teaches us that wherever we are, God is present. In heaven God is there, in hell God is there. God is anywhere we are. Jonah, a man full of pride and fear thought that by going to Tarshish instead of Nineveh he might avoid God with impunity. He could not! God is Sovereign and always present in our lives.

On the voyage to Tarshish Jonah foolishly thought he had escaped from God's presence, but God intervened. Jonah was thrown into the sea where he was swallowed by a whale, remaining in its belly for three days. Inside the whale God was also present with Jonah (Ps.139). Jonah became an Old Testament preview of Jesus' burial in the grave for three days (Matt.12:39,40).

Jonah was terrified by his burial and resurrection experience. His fear was overwhelming because of his disobedience to God. Jonah, very much like many of us, thought he could have his own way.

God is not deterred or distracted by humanistic maneuvers. The whale cast Jonah up on the shore at Nineveh where God had told Jonah to go in the first place. Can you imagine Jonah's surprise when he discovered that God was not deterred from His plan! In addition to facing the fierce Ninevites, Jonah realized with horror that his skin was bleached like a leper from the hydrochloric (digestive) acid in the whale's belly. He had deliberately disobeyed God and had become an outcast, like a leper even in his own eyes.

Despite his appearance Jonah had to face the Ninevites who were despised and considered by the Jews to be a cruel ungodly people. Prideful fear that God had sent him to witness to pagans coupled with his fear of them escalated into anger against God and the Ninevites. Jonah, whose name means "dove," previously had an excellent record as a prophet of God (2Kings14:25). Conversely, because of his disobedience to God,

Jonah now found himself on the brink of death from exhaustion due to prideful fear, anger, and depression. Confusion, another painful emotion which also includes anger, reigned supreme in Jonah's soul (mind, will, and emotions).

Can we as 40+ Christians relate to Jonah's predicament? God is similarly calling us to witness for Him in this fearsome, humanistic world in which we live. (Matt.28:19,20; Acts 1:8). Are we wasting valuable time being angry like Jonah did? Or, do we pray for God to send us forth with complete confidence and joy knowing that He can use us even more as we age beautifully and productively to proclaim the truth of Jesus as Savior and Lord?

God asked Jonah, "Is it right for you to be angry? (Jon.4:4). God confronted him with infinite patience and agape love as He does when we become discouraged and overwhelmed. Yet Jonah who was filled with pride of self; fear, and anger refused to listen to God and stated defiantly, "It is better for me to die than to live!" (Jon.4:8b) Jonah in self-righteous defiance like many of us, told God, "It is right for me to be angry even unto death!" (Jon.4:9b).

The book of Jonah ends with Jonah still angry. He placed his life on the shelf by his stubborn refusal to have his own way instead of obeying God. Jonah was immobilized by prideful fear and anger. We always lose when we like Jonah refuse to be witnesses of God's compassion and agape love. We are told by God to love all those He created including the "Ninevites" in our lives.

God offers us opportunities at 40+ to be witnesses for Him. But instead of obeying, we bemoan our age. We use age as an excuse to absent ourselves from the opportunities God gives us to live and witness to the love, joy, and peace of the Lord.

Another face of anger is manifested when we who are 40+ are labeled "childish" or "unreasonable" because of our anger. It is very difficult to rid oneself of the "angry" label when we throw temper tantrums at 40+. Significant others in our family observe this type of infantile behavior and respond accordingly. In addition, a person at 40+ who continually reacts in childish anger may unknowingly initiate feelings of helplessness, hopelessness, and despair in themselves. Hopelessness is a result of intense anger and is reflected by an appearance of sadness or sorrow. Despair and hopelessness preclude biblical relevance and may even lead to premature death.

In today's socialistic society early retirement is the indicator of success. Everything in our society is designed to make early retirement the most desirable human condition. The truth is that retirement from service to the Lord is a giant step toward early demise. Some 40+ Christians lose the joy and excitement of living in Jesus by the mere notion of being retired from their jobs. Don't let your zeal for Christ be "retired" if you retire from your occupation. The problem of unresolved anger, like Jonah allowed in himself, or a deliberate attempt to escape like Jonah keeps us from serving the Lord. Anger often overwhelms faith and results in disobedience.

The Christian alternative to fear, anger, despair, depression, and hopelessness is for us to turn to the Lord Jesus. Like the Apostle Paul we should confront the contemporary humanistic world. Through the power of the Holy Spirit we will find relevance for our lives at 40+ with biblical wisdom. Paul wrote a series of love letters to the church to encourage believers to look to Jesus, the Living Word. Paul knew from the experience of many painful rejections that Jesus is the solution to the many faces of anger. Paul turned to Jesus and learned from the Holy Spirit not to react automatically with anger (Eph.4:26-32).

Self-righteous anger is painful, unreasonable, childish, immature, unhealthy, and deadly!

Christians appear at times to be double-minded. We say we are Christians but our actions belie our talk. Think with me again about Jonah. Despite God's anointing, Jonah became self-centered and refused to surrender his anger. Even in dialogue with his loving Father, Jonah let the sun go down on his wrath (Eph. 4:26). We often allow anger to remain with us even longer as we internalize and warehouse our anger. Self-righteous anger is painful, unreasonable, childish, immature, unhealthy, and deadly!

Our lives can be seriously impaired if we react to the problem of anger without resorting to scripture for answers (Eph.4:26-32). Read and study the Bible daily. Use its practical wisdom for every angry situation you encounter.

Pray and discover what God has in store for you at 40+ as you move beyond anger to the love, joy, and peace of the Lord. You will be surprised by joy! As we age God does not want us to be arrested by fear and anger. You will be delighted by His anger free plan for your life! Being delighted in the Lord is relatively easy to say and write about but often difficult for any of us to carry out. Let us look at an example of how another face of anger was solved by our Lord.

The Lord was angry with the money changers doing business in the temple (Matt.21:12; John 2:14) and did not hesitate to express His anger. Jesus did not internalize His anger or let the sun set on His wrath (Eph.4:26). Christians must become biblically objective, not subjectively angry. We do not have to internalize the problem of anger, become depressed and thus become non-functional. Don't become part of the sickness of anger so manifest in the world.

Anger is deadly when it is internalized! It becomes emotional cancer and will spread (metastasize) throughout our mind, will, and emotions. Despair, depression, and hopelessness are symptoms of internalized cancerous anger. There is a terrible heaviness of spirit.

Do not succumb to anger, the fear of aging, or the fear of death but rather, be a dynamic witness to young people who are lost and in despair.

In addition to releasing our own anger, Christians should

offer encouragement and biblical wisdom to those who are desperate, without hope and in bondage to the problem of anger. Study and exegete specific biblical examples of anger in process in ourselves and how the Bible teaches us to respond in victory. The secular world does not have the answer for the problem of anger except to act out with more anger in the form of addictions to violence, sex and drugs.

Another face of anger is violence among young people which has resulted in a huge prison population and a rapidly rising rate of suicide among those who are severely depressed due to the problem of anger. Christians at 40+ should be

Young people are quick to observe if we live out what we say we believe. As we live out being love letters to them from God without any personal agenda, they are able by our witness to recognize they have an eternal option to abundant life in Jesus.

open to be moved by the Holy Spirit to intervene in the catastrophic loss of our young people to anger and suicide. The best example Christians can establish is to live out their lives in the love, joy, and peace of the Lord and by so doing befriend these young people who are without hope. They are your children, grandchildren, nieces and nephews, and friends. Do not succumb to anger, the fear of aging, or the fear of death but rather, be a dynamic witness to young people who are lost and in despair. Young people are quick to observe if we live out what we say we believe. As we live out being love letters to them from God without any personal agenda, they are able by our witness to recognize they have an eternal option to abundant life in Jesus.

Many mature Christians who are retired have the time to become Christians mentors for young people who are losing their lives to the problem of anger. I have often shared Jonah's story with young people. They are able to understand how Jonah's anger got him into trouble and how his depression resulted in absenting himself from God and wanting to die.

If young people feel angry and have been singled out for punishment for something they have not done, then teach them about the holy, righteous anger of the Lord Jesus Christ at sin. If you do they will learn to relate to the reality of biblical characters who have experienced what they experience today. They will benefit by relating to the Lord's solutions to their stressors and understand that Jesus has experienced everything they will ever come up against in their lives. Share with them Isaiah 53—the depth of rejection which the Lord Jesus suffered through and yet was victorious! Teach them Eph.4:26ff.

Try to be sensitive to another face of anger in the lives of your peers. Men, especially aged 55+, are particularly vulnerable to suicide. Many of these valuable men have feelings of anger expressed in attitudes of hopelessness and lack of significant purpose. Do not ignore your peers. Relate to these men in the love, joy, and peace of the Lord. Provide them with agape love and your watch care. Teach them to live abundantly in the One who is the author of life here and now and for eternity. Pray with them that Satan would not persuade them to be expendable, to abort themselves from life, but share that God has a plan for their lives. Tell them that in Jesus the best is yet to come. Point them to the self discovery sanctification process available to them in Jesus (Gal.5:22-23). Let them see joy in your life.

A problem with anger is that it is subtle like Satan. Anger manifests itself with many faces in multiple forms and strongholds (Eph.6:10ff). Anger is initiated by common everyday events and personal interactions with others. Self-initiated anger about ungodly events in our own lives is one of Satan's best kept secrets. We allow Satan to destroy us from within (Rom.7:15-25), then we project our anger onto others. As

Self-initiated anger about ungodly events in our own lives is one of Satan's best kept secrets.

our anger is being rejected by others they then get angry with us. We internalize and warehouse this anger, then become depressed. It's a vicious cycle.

The various faces of anger include some that seem downright silly and therefore relatively benign. Don't be mislead. As we age, anger may surface as minor irritations and appear superficial yet remain deeply rooted, unhealthy, and self-destructive. Pride initiates covert anger in subtle ways to the point where we deceive ourselves. An example of being silly as I age, I am tempted to make changes to keep up with the rest of the world and thereby better express who I am. Keeping up with the world as my standard is nothing less than pride. Although I think I have been aging gracefully, there is something that works within me, in psychological terms known as ego, that might compensate in some way for aging.

I needed new eyeglasses. My wife accompanied me to help select the new frames. Ann was pleased that I was doing something to change my appearance and "get with it!" She was not advocating ego, but merely expressing the hope that I was not too enmeshed by the aging process to make an effort to select stylish frames. We spent over an hour to examine various styles of frames.

Finally, I made a selection. Ann did not object because, much to her surprise, I was willing to discard my old standard frames. We both felt great that I had made a change to something different.

I wore my new glasses to Sunday School and church. I had great expectations that compliments would flow from some of my close friends. If nothing else, I thought the darker wire frames made me look younger. No "old man" gold or silver frames for me!

Not one person noticed! Silly, unhealthy, destructive anger at 76? Aging was my problem not my joy. Think about an incident in your life in which the circumstances were somewhat the same. Pride of the world led me to expect affirmation. None was forthcoming. Anger resulted. My anger was not benign. Anger took its toll. I was angry all day...even on Sunday.

Following this lack of response, I went to work on Monday and deliberately lingered at the desks of several colleagues. Again no one noticed anything different about my personal appearance. "Vanity, vanity, all is vanity" (Ecc.12:8). More silly anger on Monday.

I thought I was past caring what the world thought about my personal appearance, but I discovered that I did care. My immediate and later reaction in each case was chagrin, then anger which I internalized for later rumination (going around in circles in my mind). I was angry. Because of aging I did not feel relevant in the social groups where I thought I was significant. I grieved over the loss of significance. Later, I prayed and understood that my problem was prideful anger.

Another face of anger is the childish attempts we make to be heard. This is pride! This is raw ego! We rationalize that we need to participate in making decisions if we are to be considered relevant. God recognizes that this acting out is prideful fear to avoid rejection because of age. As we age none of us want to be ignored.

We never seem to under-stand or even contemplate that we ourselves are the problem (Gen.3:12).

Each of us continue to set up situations that we believe should result in affirmation because of our age and maturity. If affirmation is not forthcoming, we react in anger. Why do we play games to gain attention? We never seem to under-stand or even contemplate that we ourselves are the problem (Gen.3:12).

Anger is intensified in situations where we are the problem. As we age the results of anger are predictable because anger eventuates into despair, hopelessness, and depression which interferes with function.

Anger destroys our witness to others. Our countenance reflects anger which is immediately discerned by others. How we look reflects how we feel about what is going on inside of us. It is evident that although we like to think our face reflects the love of God, we appear to others to be overtly angry!

Our visible anger creates doubt in the mind and heart of the other person. We appear to be, and, are in fact, double-minded. Our relationship with God, ourselves, and signifi- cant others is thereby affected in negative ways by anger. Then anger begins to take control of our lives, and we fail to be productive for the Lord. In fact,

> *Anger begins to take control of our lives, and we fail to be productive for the Lord. In fact, some of my patients use anger as an excuse to fail. They think if they fail someone will take care of them. Even Christians use the "please rescue me syndrome" to attempt to obtain nurture instead of looking to Jesus.*

some of my patients use anger as an excuse to fail. They think if they fail someone will take care of them. Even Christians use the "please rescue me syndrome" to attempt to obtain nurture instead of looking to Jesus.

How many people in your life are you able to discern as angry people? Do you seek out angry people for fellowship or as companions? Do angry people represent Jesus? Do you see them being productive for the Lord in their witness to others? Am I one of those angry people because I am aging, i.e., 40+ ?

Although those of us who are 40+ may be able to conceal our anger, we run the risk of unresolved anger becoming a per- manent resident within us. Anger quenches the Holy Spirit. The loss of fellowship with the Holy Spirit can be deadly.

Another face of anger is the subtle paranoia (fear, persecu- tion, inordinate behavior, ungodly thoughts and ideas) that result when Christians are infected by humanistic society. Para- noia is not relieved by anything the world has to offer: entertain- ment, TV, drugs, homosexuality, promiscuity, etc. Also TV and print media on an hourly and daily basis attempt to convince us that government is the answer for mankind instead of God.

The government permits TV violence which fills the hearts and minds of the audience. The humanistic world has no answer to anger unleashed in the form of violence. The TV producers are humanists who are desperately afraid of death. Yet they are the purveyors of violence on TV. Humanists many of whom deny God are often the most aggressive presenters of anger in the form of violence.

Jesus, the Prince of love, joy, and peace is the answer to people yearning for security from anger imposed upon them by a fearful, violent, godless society. Jesus alone offers us security, "I will never desert you nor will I forsake you (Heb.13:5 NAS). Christians, especially those over 40, should be stepping up as His witnesses (Acts 1:8) of His love and security. The exciting, dynamic years of 40+ are years to model the love, joy, and peace of the Lord Jesus Christ to our violent society. We should be models for those who are fearful, angry, and in despair.

Because of its many faces, it is difficult to fully understand the problem of anger. Anger is often subtle as we have attempted to point out. Truth about anger is contained in Paul's love letter to the Ephesians. Paul identifies the problem of anger and prescribes a biblical solution (Eph.4:31-32).

We rationalize that anger is justified. However, until we repent with godly sorrow (a penitent heart) we remain arrested by anger in our spirit, mind, will, and emotions. We age much faster when anger is the chief resident in our lives. The antidote to internalized anger is to accept the reality of and personal accountability for the fact that I have a serious problem with anger. The possibility of me being the basic problem of anger should be seriously considered and given over to prayer for resolution and healing..

If in reality I confess my anger I am released to ask God to forgive me, cleanse me, and set me free from the stronghold of anger (1John1:9). Only then will I have the opportunity to show forth Jesus by my transformed life in Him (Rom.12:1,2). A joyous countenance of love and peace in the Lord is my assurance of victory over anger.

Be encouraged, life in Jesus, has only just begun! To be able to recognize and triumph over some of the less obvious faces of anger enables us to live in victory. Share your joy instead of your anger.

Psalm 96 tells us to publish the Good News of the Gospel of Jesus Christ. Is it possible that this is a literal exhortation? If so, every 40+ Christian should make contact with someone bound by the problem of anger. Pray for that person, initiate a dialogue, be a joyful witness of God's agape love, mercy, and grace. Joy precludes anger. Joy is communicable.

Many people in society are crying out for someone, any-one, to reach out to them with joy in agape love. Our great advantage at 40+ is that we can speak to them in His love from many years of God-blessed experience, the difference between being perpetually angry and the love, joy and peace of the Lord.

40+ Christians often try to distance themselves from a soci-ety that has over the years called us, with good reason, double-minded and hypocritical. We have yet to assault the bastions of hell in Jesus' name with agape love which he has commanded us to do, i.e., 'love your enemies." We have a definite advantage because of our age. As love, joy, and peace emanates from us the more the Holy Spirit prepares hearts to yield to Jesus.

This chapter has been devoted to some of the less obvious faces of anger which often prevent the 40+ Christian from engaging productively in service to our Lord Jesus Christ. God has revealed that people cannot abide with anger—it makes them a non-person a condition which the 40+ population seeks to avoid.

Being a non-person is painful. We are surrounded in our society by people for whom there has been no answer to the problem of anger. In Jesus, at 40+ we can be God's messengers to reveal anger for the danger it is to Christians and non-

Christians alike. Jesus says "be angry and sin not, do not let the sun go down on your anger." (Eph.4:26). Internalized anger is dangerous to a persons health and well-being. It should not be ignored. The love, joy, and peace of the Lord is the recommended treatment plan for anger.

Internalized anger is dangerous to a persons health and well-being.

In the next chapter "Without Jesus it is Boring to Grow Old!" I address one of the most virulent and least understood faces of anger. Boredom at 40+ is a facade for despair, fear, and aloneness with specific regard to the aging process (crucifixion of the body).

Take a few minutes to love yourself enough to answer the following questions on the application and accountability page which follows. These questions and your answers may provide needed insight for application of your faith. Accountability is essential to good spiritual health.

If you have been wasting time and energy by being overwhelmed by anger or are totally unaware that anger may be the reason for your malaise, these questions and scripture may enlighten your life.

Do I have a problem with anger? ❑ Yes   0 - 10____
Describe your response and be very specific.

Am I like Jonah? ❑ Yes   0 - 10____   ❑ No

If the answer is no, describe yourself in one word

_____.

Now describe yourself in one paragraph using your one-word description of yourself as the basis for your perspective. Pray that the Lord will give you insight and enlightenment (2Pet.3:18).

How many hours of the week does the negative liberal media impact your life?____

There are 168 hours in a week (24 X 7). Do you tithe 10% of your time to the Lord or to TV?
Hours in a week watching TV?____
Hours in Bible study and prayer?____

Do these questions make you angry?
If the answer is yes explain why? It may help you to deal with your anger in the power of the Holy Spirit.

Dying to Live Abundantly at 40+ is a spiritual primer to encourage you in the application of your life to be consistent with what God designed you to be— the image and likeness of His Son Jesus. This book can be a self-discovery paradigm, an exciting way to understand God's plan for your life at 40+, here and now and for eternity with Him.

Be encouraged! *Seek ye first the Kingdom of God and His righteousness and all these things will be added unto you.*

MATTHEW 6:33

RECOMMENDED SCRIPTURE READING:
Ephesians 4:23-32
2 Corinthians 4:8-18; 5:1-8

CHAPTER 4

〰️

Without Jesus it is Boring to Grow Old!

Seek first the Kingdom of God and His righteousness and all these things shall be added unto you.

MATTHEW 6:33

Aperson's perspective on aging and the dying and death process is determined by his/her relationship with Jesus Christ as Lord and Savior. A negative perspective about aging inevitably develops without Jesus Christ because His biblical absolutes bring joy to aging. Negativism, which often eventuates as a result of perceived social rejection or self-rejection, or both, is bred from anger and hopelessness and leads to boredom and feelings of not being relevant.

E. Kubler-Ross, M.D. (1969), delineated the stages of dying and death. These five stages (responses), have been generally accepted as the rites of passage when a terminal illness is diagnosed. (graphics mine)

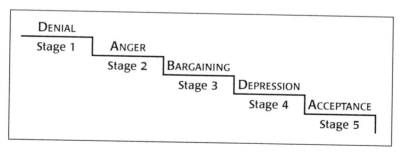

When a person without Jesus Christ in his life is diagnosed with a terminal disease the five stages in the process of dying and death are manifested in mental and emotional rites of passage. However, when dying and death are in process but a person is free from any physical disease, i.e., aging the rites of passage are not clearly defined.

Without Jesus Christ, our competitive, fast moving secular humanistic society may impose stress on the aging in the form of social rejection to the point of initiating the process of dying and death just like a terminal disease does. Social rejection can lead to boredom. Although it has not been identified as a terminal disease, boredom can be just as deadly. Boredom, because of its subtlety can remain as undetected as hypertension, another silent killer.

For the aged, the rites of passage of dying and death without physical terminal disease are rarely discussed or defined. For those without Jesus Christ in contemporary secular society the process of aging is something that is despised, feared, dreaded, and to be delayed at any cost! People attempt to ignore aging and society does not care. In contrast to aging, youth is worshipped, adored, and idolized, despite the fact that youth is fleeting and everyone inevitably ages!

Boredom at any age, may encroach on our lives like an insidious termite infestation and is especially dangerous to our health as we age. Boredom in secular society is a judgment made by man about himself. Judgment of self and others is forbidden in the Bible (Matt. 7:1 KJV). God is excluded. Man in a strictly humanist environment over the course of history has arbitrarily decided the aged have little value or relevancy in society. This has led to the terminal disease of boredom.

In the late 1950s, 60s, and 70s those who were considered elderly (anyone over 30) were not seen as relevant. They were over the hill! Parents and grandparents were bored and frustrated with angry rebellion so they collapsed into permissiveness. They were too busy trying to make up the money lost during WWII so they did not take time to comfort their children and teach them biblical absolutes. The irony of disobedience to biblical absolutes (which we in the 65+ group failed to live and impart to our children) is a cancerous legacy that the flower children of the 60's rebellion inherited.

The 60's revolutionaries had some well founded complaints against their 40+ parents but instead of pleading their case to God in Jesus' name to establish His righteousness in their lives, they chose to reject God's law. In their rebellion they substituted the humanistic manifesto that each man/woman is his/her own god. Today the former hippies are paying a terrible price through the behavior of their children, each of whom have similarly become their own god

During the last twenty years parents and grandparents have come into my office agonizing about the tragedy of AIDS, drug addiction, abortion, and many other forms of social anarchy acted out by their children. Much of this acting out is directed against parents and grandparents in defiance of biblical order. The 60's generation are now faced with the same arrogance in their own children as they acted out against their parents and grandparents. The former hippies are now in the "over the hill" group. However, their children, the present day "here and now generation" have given the hippie generation more trouble and heartaches than the hippies ever gave their parents. The strongholds of arrogance and rebellion which the 60's generation initiated is now being used against them by their own children. The former 60's hippies are not considered relevant today by their children! The 60's hippies feel hopeless.

The infirm, the homeless, the disadvantaged, and the aged, including those with biblical family absolutes, are also virtually ignored in today's society. These groups may be described as dying from being bored. They are frightened and weak. There are millions of Americans in name only, who are disenfranchised by age. For them, without Jesus it is boring to grow old. They are powerless.

A group who are bored to distraction are those persons who are 50+ yet able to function well at the peak of their performance, based upon years of experience. However, many of these 50+ people are fired from their jobs because in today's society they are considered "aged." They are replaced by inexperienced younger men and women who are paid less, but are hired because they are younger, more energetic, more attractive. The here and now generation are in demand and the late 40+ and 50+ people are summarily rejected.

Throughout the world, there is an increasing societal trend toward rejection of 55+ persons who attempt to avail themselves of health care services. For example the national health plan in several major countries of the world do not include or provide for people 55+ who have serious illness. Surgery and other expensive medical procedures are denied the elderly despite the fact that they have great potential for productive longevity as life expectancy increases.

The arrogance of social elitists' legislation fails to prevent discrimination against the elderly, except when elections approach. Except for obtaining their vote, the elitists attitude is "why waste time and money on the elderly?" They are nice to have around as progenitors of long life in the family, but the elderly in reality are only to be tolerated. Basically, they are a financial burden and essentially useless. "We are just too busy! We do not have time to take care of them!"

Another group of elderly persons are at the center of a debate surrounding the ethics of euthanasia. Almost imperceptibly God's law is being displaced by the pluralism of humanistic man/woman, each of whom is their own god. The plague of abortion, legislated killing of human life by civil law for which God will hold us accountable, has established a basis for the increasing predisposition toward doctor-assisted death on demand. God, the creator of life, is now displaced by persons who are their own god thus the self-appointed legislators of the lives of the elderly when it comes to time

Boredom arises out of a person's perceived lack of the God-given right to live free from rejection.

and method of death. Is it any wonder that the aged are suffocating from rejection that eventuates into boredom? "No one wants us because we are old".

The aged are increasingly aware that the wisdom and respect previously accorded them from years of life experience has been displaced by the envy and anger of humanists who are elitist power brokers. Arrogance, expressed as lack of respect toward those who are 40+ is clearly evident today. They feel rejected, hopeless, useless and that leads to deadly boredom.

Without Jesus, without His purpose for our lives, without His Holy Spirit's power, anger, in its many godless, overt, and covert forms, makes life truly boring. Boredom arises out of a person's perceived lack of the God-given right to live free from rejection.

Boredom is synonymous with hopelessness, which can lead to death. Anomie, the blank stare of hopelessness, covers the faces of many older citizens today. Deadly boredom entices

Boredom is imperceptible. Suicide is similarly undetected.

many 40+ persons to become unduly preoccupied with physical illness. Death is usually attributed to physical illness. However, boredom due to rejection from family, significant others, and contemporary society—"I am depressed because I have no place or significance in society"—is also life-threatening. As the emotional pain of rejection is experienced hopelessness follows. Inability to renew a right spirit within you through Jesus results in a daily boring "nothingness" routine in life.

Boredom is imperceptible, not easily identified even by helping professionals. Family and significant others who think they are attuned to those who are 40, 50, 60, 70, 80, 90, and 100+ rarely discern boredom in process. Suicide is similarly undetected.

Boredom is a form of emotional cancer. I diagnose it as "boredoma" which spreads, and remains undetected even by the person who is experiencing being bored to death. Untold thousands who are 40+ suffer from rejection and life-threatening "boredoma." They have concluded that the freedom to live freely, productively, and independently in a socialistic humanist society is impossible.

Boredom is a form of emotional cancer.

Some people especially feel this social rejection and are prone to boredom. Societal rejection particularly affects individuals who are only children. The only child syndrome can make for a difficult journey through life. The lack of siblings in childhood, youth, early and later adulthood take an extra toll at 40+. Society often makes the assumption that an only child has benefits that do not accrue to families in which there are two or more children. It is true that for the only child there is no competition for attention and affection from parents; however, it is also true that an only child does not enjoy the comfort of sibling companionship and security early on. Sibling communication, which can be essential to long life and personal security, is absent as they age.

Societal discrimination toward the aged person, who is an only child at 50, 60, 70+ may have devastating effects. I know a number of people in this situation who feel they have nowhere to turn for comfort from the anger and fear they experience because of rejection. There is no sibling support. Without Jesus to provide comfort through prayer, the Bible and His Holy Spirit, helplessness, immobility, boredom, and death follow.

The aging single and single-again persons are another group who represent a segment of the population that are in danger of dying of boredom. They, like the only child group, have difficulty in establishing significant relationships. If you are over 40 in this society you are conditioned to feel that you simply do not fit in! The 40+ singles and singles again are jarred into reality that they have been used but not accepted. Social rejection is not their singleness which is painfully real to them but their age which is judged to be "over the hill." The label of being "40" means excommunication from society and is destructive because it exacerbates aging.

There is another group of older men (70-80+) who are at risk of being bored to death. This group consists of men who despite the fact they are in a family seem to separate themselves because of age. Many of their peers have predeceased them, and these men feel they do not have an active family interest to engage them as females do, i.e., my Mother. She involved herself in the lives of her children, grandchildren, great-grandchildren, and a great-great-grandchild. But these older men are inclined to forget (if they ever knew) the biblical exhortation to maintain the patriarchal position with their immediate and extended family. The grandfather role provides great comfort and security to family members (Prov. 31). As patriarchs these men should be the image of God the Father (Gen.1:26.27), our great and ageless Holy Comforter who provides dignity, protection and eternal security for His children.

Slowly, almost imperceptibly, these older men who become bored with aging then slip into a "separateness mode" like an old lion or bear. Even though they reside with the family they have wandered off into the wilderness and aloneness of boredom. To these men I issue a word of caution. Unless and until God relieves you of your role as priest, prophet, elder, father, grandfather, great-grandfather, beware of neglecting your God-given role and acountability. Cancerous "boredoma" is life threatening. God has not excused any male, despite his age, who claims Jesus as Lord and Savior to be retired, separate, and bored to death. Abraham, Caleb, Moses, and many others all overcame great adversity by God's grace. Each of these men of God lived to be well over 100 years of age. None of them were reported to be bored or retired from productive service for God.

The debilitating pain of aging from boredom as a result of self and social rejection negatively impacts our physical condition. In addition to emotional pain the importance of stress initiated by aging, without hope for the present or future is significant. Without Jesus, without His Holy Spirit to comfort, encourage, and sustain us with the joy of aging (John 3:16) knowing that our lives in Jesus have only just begun, physical illness with emotional overlay may appear to be benign but is in fact deadly.

But there is freedom from boredom. My thesis is, "Without Jesus it is boring to grow old." Without Jesus it is dangerous to your health to grow old. To illustrate the importance of seeking Jesus and the Kingdom of God and His righteousness as we age let us look at a well accepted humanist model of the stages of dying. The humanist model ends in death without any promise, suggestion, or intimation of eternal life. These humanist constructs, such as the Kubler-Ross model, are without hope, without eternal life, without resurrection.

In the Kubler-Ross model, the five stages of dying are intensely painful, hopeless, and boring. Kubler-Ross accurately presents the humanist rites of passage for death. These rites of passage are devoid of any hope of resurrection (John 3:16) as death becomes imminent. Resurrection and eternal life are not mentioned.

Denial, the first stage may help relieve the trauma of physical illness for a short time. However, denial is fleeting in the face of medical test results. Anger, the second stage, is resident in denial and may also for a short period of time allow a person to ventilate or introject the reality of their illness. Projecting anger on others and becoming preoccupied with intense anger may temporarily avoid the necessity of acknowledging the seriousness of your illness. Denial and anger are not therapeutic. They are costly measured by self-imposed debilitating stress because denial is only a defense against reality.

Stage One denial and Stage Two anger only delay emotional pain and suffering for as long as one can maintain a facade to avoid reality. The facade crumbles as denial and anger indicate the lack of biblical strength and hope.

Stage Three is bargaining which involves negotiation with

God about postponing death. If God, or other power in which the dying person believes, "will spare me, then I will do for God or other power whatever is required." How sad that the remainder of life should be reduced to bargaining with God. Bargaining is tragic especially for humanists who have deliberately ignored, rejected, or never taken time to acknowledge God and put their trust in Him.

Denial, anger, and bargaining become extremely boring at some point in the dying process. I have observed humanists who throughout their lives have ignored or denied God, yet in extremis are reduced to bargaining with God for their lives. These humanists never cry out for Marx, politicians, legislators, or other gurus, nor do they cry out to the socialist elitists. They cry out like all human beings who are in the process of dying in the loneliest of experiences. They cry out in terror and attempt to bargain with God (Ps.73).

The Fourth Stage of the Kubler-Ross model is a psychosocial and medical disease. Depression in the dying and death process in my clinical experience most often is anger turned inward on oneself. Depression as pointed out previously is a form of emotional cancer. Emotional cancer spreads rapidly and engulfs the person who is in the process of being ejected from life. The process of dying appears to be more rapid when a person is depressed.

Without Jesus it is boring to grow old, then die. Dying without hope for the future is boring!

Surprisingly, depression at times may relieve the pain of physical illness. Depression may act on the human psyche like a psychological anesthesia. Nevertheless, depression retains its own identity as an addictive emotional illness. Depression may be life-threatening yet secondary to a primary physical illness.

Acceptance, the final stage in the Kubler-Ross model sounds peaceable, but is in fact boring. The rites of passage through the stages of dying and death are in and of themselves intensely painful and unrewarding. Acceptance might suggest a positive dimension to dying and death. It is not! Without Jesus it is boring to grow old, then die. Dying without hope for the future is boring!

Without Jesus, the Fifth Stage of dying and death, acceptance, could be described as voluntary resignation from life. How unnecessary, what a waste, how eternally tragic!

Rejection of the aged by a humanistic world, permitted by the aged, exacerbated by illness, either physical or emotional, or both, is the summit of boredom. Without Jesus, the Fifth Stage of dying and death, acceptance, could be described as voluntary resignation from life. How unnecessary, what a waste, how eternally tragic!

Thank God for Jesus who is the eternal living alternative to death. God provides in Jesus five stages of living. These stages are living reality— the biblical norm for those in Jesus whether they suffer from physical, emotional illness or very old age like my mother at 98+. These five stages of living in reality are contained in John 3:16 (paraphrased), and are the God-ordained stages of His provision for each one of us. They are not boring. The future for us in Jesus Christ is dynamic and filled with the excitement of love, joy, and peace.

The Five Biblical Stages of Eternal Life:

1) God so loved the world (everyone, without any discrimination)

2) that God gave His only begotten son Jesus,

3) that whosoever believeth in Him,

4) will not perish

5) but will have everlasting life, will never die for all time and eternity.

People of all ages have heard this biblical message of eternal life which is for us to reside in heaven with Jesus. However, many have chosen to refuse or ignore God's invitation. God's gift of Jesus Christ is out of His agape love for us, so that we may have the gift of eternal life to be wih God forever. The Bible clearly states that the moment you give your life to Jesus, eternal life begins (John 3:16). Aging, dying and death are swallowed up in light of:

1) Our God-given soul/personality, our individual identity (mind, will, and emotions) which has been designed by God to live in heaven with Jesus for all time and eternity. Reconciliation is provided for us by God through the death and resurrection of His Son (2 Cor. 5:17-24).

2) Our God-designed soul/personality (mind, will, and emotions) which is centered in Jesus Christ will live in a heavenly body forever. We will never become sick or perish. Dying and death will never be a fearful issue for the resurrected Christian. God by His love, grace, and mercy has granted us eternal life!

We will have wonderful new bodies in heaven, homes that will be ours forever, made for us by God Himself, and not by human hands. How weary we grow of our present bodies. That is why we look forward eagerly to the day when we shall have heavenly bodies which we shall put on like new clothes. For we shall not be merely spirits without bodies.

2 CORINTHIANS 5:1-3 TLB

3) We will have relevancy as we praise, worship, and adore God.

4) Jesus has overcome our pain, boredom, and death and has given us eternal life.

5) Physical and emotional death is unknown in heaven. Sin was generated on earth, and wages of sin, which is

death, have been overcome by Jesus' victory over death evidenced by His bodily resurrection and then His ascension into heaven (John 11:25; 1 John 5:4; 1 Cor. 15:54).

How can we occupy our time here on earth until we see Jesus face to face in heaven? The answer to that question is living for His purpose for our lives. His purpose for us is to live without boredom in the love, joy, and peace of the Lord at any age, but especially for those 40+. These years of aging are beautiful and can be the most exciting time we will ever experience here on earth. St. Paul in his epistles, explains biblical truth to us as biblical absolutes basic to dying (crucifixion) then living for eternity (resurrection).

> *For me living means opportunities for Christ, and dying— well, that is better yet. But if living will give me more opportunities to win people to Christ, then I really don't know which is better, to live or die! But the fact is that I can be of more help to you by staying! Yes, I am still needed down here and so I feel certain I will be staying on earth a little longer, to help you grow and become happy in your faith. My staying will make you glad and give you reason to glorify Christ Jesus for keeping me safe, when I return to visit you again.*
>
> PHILIPPIANS 1:21-26 TLB

Since God in Jesus Christ is in control of my life then boredom, despair, depression, and dying are not options for me. I live, move, and have my being by the grace of God only! His plan for Christians began before the beginning of time and is operational today (Ps.139; Eph.1:3-12). St. Paul drew this same conclusion in his letter to the Phillipians.

But the fact is that I can be of more help to you by staying.

Like Paul, I rejoice that there is work for me to do here on earth. I enjoy being about my Father's business. At 76 I rejoice when I awaken, delighted to discover I am still breathing! I feel the strong beat of my heart. I am able to move around one day at a time and enjoy my being here for Jesus' purpose for my life. God equips me to function everyday in His plan and service. No longer am I in control of my life. What a blessing each day to turn over control of my life to God. He is able to handle any of my problems with infinite wisdom and power by His love, mercy, and grace! He is my living reality now and forever. I am delighted and surprised each day by joy.

God supplies my every need out of His bounty. For example, as important as my wife, children, family, and colleagues are, they do not provide oxygen essential for life, nor the lungs to breathe oxygen. If you think about something as seemingly simple as breathing which has always been taken for granted, you quickly arrive at the conclusion—God is in control! Have you ever been out in the fresh air and thanked God for the ability to breathe and the oxygen he gives us to breathe. God is my life and my provider. Praise His name.

By His infinite grace, my heart beats and pumps blood enriched with oxygen and nutrients to maintain my physical and mental well-being. Clearly my basic ability to function and grow as a person rests with God alone plus nothing. I am in the good hands of The Great Creator and Physician. What a blessing!

Our energy and concentration while we are here on earth should focus on the reality of God's purpose for our lives here and now. What would God have us do to bring His kingdom here on earth as it is in heaven?" (Matt. 6:10). Christians should never be bored, but instead be dynamic witnesses. God has a full agenda for us at any age, especially at 40+ as our children leave home. These are exciting and dynamic times in which we can be fully and productively occupied in obedient service to our Lord and Savior Jesus Christ And He will reveal Himself to us (John 14:21,23).

The Bible tells us to buy up every opportunity and be busy about our Father's business until He returns to take us to be with Him. Praise God, His wonderful plan for us at 40, 50, 60, 70, 80, 90, 100+ is to occupy till He comes. Occupy with the exhortation to "Rejoice evermore, pray without ceasing, in everything give thanks for this is the will of God in Christ Jesus for you" (1 Thess. 5:16-18).

I am trying to put this plan into effect in my own life. In order to be fit to occupy myself in the Great Commission (Matt. 28:19,20; John 15:17; Acts 1:8) I am involved in running. I never ran track until I was 66 when I joined a physical fitness program at Duke University Medical Center which provided facilities for seniors in a medically supervised environment. For the first nine months I engaged in all the daily routines of the program. By that time I was able to run six laps of a quarter mile track—a total of 1 1/2 miles—I felt like a new man! My weight and blood pressure were significantly lowered as well and I was not bored.

Subsequent to that time by God's grace I was able to enter into regional track events for seniors and finally reached the state level of competition. Three years later I competed at the U.S. National level in the 50-meter breaststroke event. Two years later at 71, I qualified to compete again at the National Senior Olympics in the 1500-meter track event posting the best time I had ever run and coming in 12th out of 15 national competitors. I was delighted to be able to finish in that level of competition!

This accomplishment was of great significance for me. As I completed the last lap of the race I saw something as I approached the finish line. Although the spectators cheered for everyone, even those of us who brought up the rear, I did not even hear the cheers. God had a greater blessing in store for me. What I did see and hear was:

Therefore we also, since we are surrounded by so great a cloud of witnesses, let us lay aside every weight, and the sin (without Jesus it is boring to grow old) which so easily ensnares us, let us run with endurance the race that is set

before us, looking unto Jesus, the author and finisher of
our faith who for the joy that was set before Him endured
the cross, despising the shame, and has sat down at the
right hand of the throne of God.

I know God alone granted me the strength to run in the U.S. National Senior Olympics. Then He gave me the insight provided by the Holy Spirit to understand the meaning of this event for my life in Him. At the finish line, tired as I was, the vision God gave me of those witnesses made an impression on me that I shall never forget. The message I received from God at 71 was to occupy my time by running the race with the love, joy, and peace of the Lord and thereby fulfill the Great Commission (Matt. 28:19,20; Acts 1:8).

God enabled me to run and swim by His strength and power. He demonstrated to me that all things are possible in Him. In sharing these events I prayerfully suggest to you that by seeking the Kingdom of God and His righteousness (Matt.6:33), you will eliminate any possibility of being bored. In fact, in Jesus all things necessary for you to occupy yourself in His service will be added unto you. None of the events in your life are boring to Him.

Another blessing God has bestowed on me to avoid being bored is not being able to retire. In my early career following four years in the Marines during World War II, I worked for a small company that did not have a retirement plan. After 23 years with this company, the Lord led me to resign as a vice president and director to complete my education. For 11 years—from age 51 to 62—I pursued my education. My career change was wonderfully directed and managed by God. During the final year of my masters degree requirements I worked as a research and clinical associate at a major university medical center. Upon the completion of my internship I joined a Christian medical practice as a medical psychologist. Following this clinical experience I entered private practice as a Christian counselor/ psychologist. None of these regimens included a retirement plan, so I have never been able to retire. Retirement is not His plan for my life in service to Him! Yet God (who is also not retired) provides for me and my wife by His love and grace. I continue to seek His Kingdom here on earth by writing and publishing the Good News (Ps. 96). I also teach, advise, and have a counseling practice. God is faithful and never fails to meet our needs.

I can say that from time to time I do long to slow down, but those feelings pass quickly and are supplanted by more opportunities for self-discovery than I can handle. I continue to occupy myself enthusiastically in a self-discovery process and paradigm which is very exciting! My zest for life in Jesus here and now and for eternity is all pervasive. At 76, I have not as yet begun to discover all that God designed me to be and then do. Being in Jesus I am

My thesis, "Without Jesus it is boring to grow old!" is based upon my exciting apprenticeship for eternity. Apprenticeship at 76 is associated with being youthful, a new beginning, yet retaining the blessings of age in the love, joy, and peace of the Lord. I like that!

enabled above all other vital considerations to do His perfect will for my life. With Jesus as my model, it has been my experience that boredom is impossible.

My constant preoccupation is to seek the kingdom of God and His righteousness. Like a little child I am delighted with the potential God has given me to answer the questions of:

Who am I? (in Jesus)

Why am I here? What is the purpose of my life in Jesus?

*Where have I come from and where I am going?*1

My thesis, "Without Jesus it is boring to grow old!" is based upon my exciting apprenticeship for eternity. Apprenticeship at 76 is associated with being youthful, a new beginning, yet retaining the blessings of age in the love, joy, and peace of the Lord. I like that!

At 76 it has become my time to begin to exercise and to develop my spiritual gifts from God. Then to use these gifts for His honor and glory. Love, joy, peace, and patience are coming more and more into focus. Patience (of which I have had little in the past) has become a form of endurance like running a race—the endurance to prevail. Gentleness, goodness, and faithfulness are becoming more manifest in my life with each passing day. I see evidence in my relationships at home and in my work that sanctification is in process (Gal. 5:22-23).

Without Jesus it is boring to grow old. Jesus living within us will enable Christians to fulfill God's mission for their lives. Each person God created is to become Christ-Centered[1] in obedience to His Word. Then the love, joy, and peace of the Lord will fully occupy you with His purpose for your individual, unique, important life in service to Him. Take time to discover what a great job God has done in creating you for His eternal purpose. Break out of boredom by His Grace and discover His exciting, dynamic, healthy will for your life.

Eye has not seen, nor ear heard, nor mind conceived what God has prepared for those who love Him.
1 CORINTHIANS 2:9

So seek ye first the Kingdom of God and His righteousness and all these things shall be added unto you.
MATTHEW 6:33

Don't be bored! Be real. Be alive and well in Jesus for all time and eternity!

---

[1] Christ-Centered Personality Development, Dr. Robert Abarno, ©1988. Second Edition 1992, Third Edition 1994, Fourth Edition 1996. All rights reserved.

Are you a Christian ? ❑ Yes   ❑ No
Do you believe in the inerrant Word of God? ❑ Yes ❑ No
Are you bored? 0-10 ____
Are you in one of the five stages of dying? ❑ Yes, Stage ____
Are you in one of the five stages of living? ❑ Yes, Stage ____

What spiritual gifts are being developed in you as you age?

•

•

•

•

Are you prayerfully and actively using these gifts?
    ❑ Yes ❑ No
    If yes, how? (Describe in a few sentences).

    If not, why not?

    Share with others and encourage them to enjoy aging in the process of sanctification in Jesus.

    Suggest to others that their lives as they age may be the very best time to speak, write, sing, and publish the Good News of Jesus (Ps. 96 TLB).

    Remember as you age that you are in good company with God. Eternal life has only just begun! Jesus is alive and well and He loves you. As you age focus on these biblical truths of life.

CHAPTER 5

Jim and Laura – At 40+
They Have Only Just Begun

Jim and Laura are good examples at 40+ of personal self-discovery in the love, joy, and peace of the Lord. Jim is 41, and Laura is 40. They have three children: Jeff 15, Mary 13, and Sally 10. This family represents a composite of my patients who have been seen in counseling over the past twenty years. As with other couples struggling with marital and family relationships who attempt to live as Christians, I thought Jim and Laura's problems were confined to their individual genetic and developmental personalities. During the years of my practice as a Christian therapist I realized how damaging process philosophy is in the form of godless humanism. Then, how humanism has negatively impacted American culture and families. The encroachment of rationalism, dualism, and socialism which are the opposite of biblical absolutes, have insidiously undermined American life. Marriages and families have been negatively affected! America was initially constituted as a Christian nation ("In God we trust").

However, many of the framers of our Constitution were not biblical Christians, but rationalists. Rationalism has made significant, long lasting inroads in American life. The early church in America was not immune to rationalism which was ingested and then evenuated into evangelicalism even in those churches who believed in the inerrant Word of God. The compromise came, as it did earlier in church history with Aquinas, in that rationalism was perceived as related to or a part of Christianity. In the 1700s rationalism in America under the guise of evangelical Christianity eventuated into Western world evangelicalism. Biblical Christianity was shunted aside in favor of evangelicalism.

The problems Jim and Laura encountered as a family have been rampant in America since the late 1700s. Big government known as Fabian socialism, legislates what is claimed to be best for the American family. Maternalism/socialism have captured American government, society, and church. Politicians who are the priestess's of maternalistic big government empower themselves over the people. "We know what is best for the people."

Thus government elitists instead of parents have legislated and adjudicated themselves to power over the family. They impose woman's law as king (Lex Rex), thus supplanting God's law as King (Rex Lex). Biblical absolutes as the order of life for individuals and families has been

God always wins in the end!

trashed by rationalism/socialism. Biblical Americans despair under government control of their lives until they realize and are comforted by the fact of history that God always wins in the end!

Families like Jim, Laura, and their children have been caught up in this maelstrom of godless socialism. Judeo-Christian biblical absolutes are mocked by the humanist world. The result of a socialist permissive society of nihilistic young people has seriously eroded the American family structure and God-given parental authority. Persecution of biblical Christianity is overt and unrestrained in violation of the Constitution and the Bill of Rights.

Jim and Laura are at the threshold of the aging process at 40+. They are attempting to maintain a Christian perspective in the lives of their children in the midst of worldly confusion. Despite their faith, they represent contemporary society in its busy hedonistic preoccupation with worldly image. They have allowed themselves to be completely deluded, unaware of evangelicalism in the church which is a humanistic departure from biblical Christianity.

Humanism/rationalism, socialism and the lack of biblical Christianity impacted this family. I first encountered them when, at Laura's request, she and Jim came to my office with a chief complaint of a lack of family intimacy. Jim is a busy attorney who is required to work long hours each day. Laura is wife, mother, and full-time homemaker. With three children and a husband who is rarely at home, Laura is always stressed attempting to meet the demands of her multiple roles. As the principal caretaker, she is constantly exposed to the behavior of the children who reflect a permissive humanistic society which contests the biblical absolutes of God on a daily basis.

Jeff is a rebellious 15 year old teenager. He has remained away from home on several occasions which confused and worried his mother and father. He became a complete mystery to his parents. His sisters are frightened by Jeff's behavior. Yet Mary and Sally have similarly cut off communication with their mother. They lock the door when they are on the telephone. They are reluctant to confide in their mother. Their father is never available when the children have a need to speak with him about their lives.

Laura is fearful about what is happening to her family. Jim and Laura say they are Christians, but like many others in contemporary society their family life resonates with trauma. Evangelicalism in their church reinforces the busyness and activity rampant in the world in which they attempt to function. The humanism of the world mesmerizes them so much that sharing time as a family is non-existent.

Jim, the busy overburdened attorney, comes home late and is totally exhausted. There is no time for loving greetings, hugs or family devotions. When Jim arrives home he cross-examines Laura and the children, then judges them by their frightened responses. Laura has to repeatedly point out to Jim that she and the children are not defendants in a courtroom. The childrens response is Jeff's rebellion and the girls' evasiveness which induce fear and then anger in Laura. Her anger is projected onto Jim, herself and God.

Laura has a masters degree in social work. Despite the advantage of an education which is related to family problems,

Laura's chaotic parental history has also affected Jim, Jeff, Mary, and Sally. Communication among family members is essentially non-existent. The urgency of schedule and demands of contemporary secular society have displaced biblical order in this family.

The disunity Laura experiences reminds her of the environment in which she grew up. Her mother and father argued continuously in front of her and her siblings. Laura's life with Jim is similarly out of biblical order (Col. 3:18-21: Eph. 5:22-33). This is not what Laura expected in a "Christian" marriage.

Jim also had a difficult time growing up without nurture from mother or father. Jim's father was a very successful attorney. Jim has been fearful all of his life that he would not become a well-known attorney like his father. His preoccupation with this fear of failure to be like Dad distracted him from establishing a secure Christian home with Laura. His first priority of being a highly respected well known attorney is out of biblical order (Matt. 22:37-39).

A clinical review discloses we have in this counseling process a vigorous middle-class family who are burdened about the lack of biblical order in their lives. Due to the inadequacy of family communication Laura and Jim sought out a Christian counselor. They decided to obtain biblical insight to break the self-centered hysterical cycle of the humanistic world in which they live. Their marital and family relationships are critical. Biblical absolutes in this family have been eroded by the unremitting pressure of a busy world.

However, Jim and Laura remain convinced that the Bible contains the answers to all problems of mankind, including individual and family problems they are encountering. "We have the mind of Christ" (1 Cor. 2:16), and, "eye has not seen, nor ear heard, nor have entered into the heart of man the things that God has prepared for those who love Him" (1 Cor. 2:9).

In our first counseling session we prayed and then reaffirmed that the family is the Christian church in miniature. Biblically, the husband/father has the role of pastor/leader. The wife/mother is his revered companion. The children are the congregation. The authority of the father and mother rests upon their individual and corporate faith in Jesus Christ as Savior and Lord. Submission to the Holy Spirit and obedience to the absolutes of the Bible complete the protocol for the Christian family. Jim and Laura covenanted together that this protocol is the biblical order for them as a Christian family.

As they grew up, neither Jim or Laura had experienced biblical order in their families. When Jeff, Mary, and Sally began to draw away from them, old memories from the past resulted in Jim and Laura yielding to the world instead of to the Word of God. Jim and Laura did not want to risk losing their children to a secular humanistic society so they agreed to seek help.

In addition, as Jim and Laura realized they were at the 40+ stage ("over the hill") they became frightened for themselves and their children. What if they felt they were becoming too old and unable to relate to their children? They did not understand, as many 40+ parents do not understand, that life for them in Jesus had only just begun!

40+ are the years of adventure and self-discovery that the Bible describes and the world ignores. The Bible is replete with people who began to find out, "Who am I and why am I here?" at 40. They are the people who continue to be productive in their lives for God and themselves. For example, Moses lived out three 40-year stages of life. The Lord took Moses at 120 while he was still clear-eyed and vigorous. Just like Jim and Laura, Moses had problems in his marriage and also in relationships leading the Jews into the promised land. Moses who God described as His friend had a life full of new beginnings with many problems, but he always turned to God.

In counseling, I referred Jim and Laura to the Bible as the manual for a marriage to be in biblical order, and to help reconcile their family. Individual and family roles are clearly defined in the Bible. Jim had failed to lead his little family (church) biblically. Instead he had made his law practice his church. Jim attempted to emulate his father instead of Jesus. When he realized he was paying homage to the world of man's law instead of the law of God and the biblical needs of his family, Jim was able to reconstruct his busy schedule. He began to tithe his time to the Lord, Laura, and the children.[1]

As the counseling process continued it became effective when individual and family devotions were engaged in on a daily basis. For the first time meaningful communication between family members began to replace angry defensive responses. Problems were presented at family devotions and prayed for with well-documented results. Praise and worship replaced fear and anger. Biblical order and family unity were not achieved immediately (Rom. 12:1-2); however, the Holy Spirit of God prevailed and the results over time were evident.

Jeff began to spend time talking with his Dad after family devotions, and Jim took time to listen. Laura observed communication taking place between them and wisely did not ask to be included. Jeff gave up staying out and came home every night. Nothing was said about his change in behavior, but it was evident even to his sisters that Jeff was no longer in rebellion. Jeff set an example for his sisters so that they included their mother in their "girl talks" and no longer evaded Laura's questions or locked their door when they were on the telephone.

Mary led one of her girlfriends to the Lord while at home during a Bible study in which Laura was the teacher. Jane had always admired and respected Mary. She saw Mary as the "ideal teenager," but was not aware of the turmoil in Mary's home. Mary shared with Jane that she was not the "ideal teenager" and in fact recently had to change her behavior toward her mother and father. Jane was impressed by Mary's openness and sensed by Holy Spirit insight that her own personal decision for Jesus was real!

Laura followed Mary's example when she presented Jesus

---

1   Christ-Centered Personality Development, Dr. Robert Abarno, ©1988. Second Edition 1992, Third Edition 1994, Fourth Edition 1996. All rights reserved.

to her next door neighbor who had just been divorced. Laura and Jean had been friends for years. This lady was shocked when Laura shared that being married to Jim was like being single. Jean thought Laura had the best of all husbands in Jim and that her children were under control. Jean finally responded to Jesus because she began to see a very consistent change in Laura's life.

Jim and Laura dealt with the problem of fear of failure. They began to understand that the problem of anger toward their parents had a negative effect on their own relationship. Arguing in front of the children and not measuring up to significant others' expectations of them had seriously endangered their marriage. They began to be each other's personal prayer partner and share their deepest thoughts and feelings together in prayer. The problem they originally presented in counseling, a lack of intimacy, was no longer a problem since they had become biblically intimate. They stated to me they were now best friends.

Finally, as we prayed and worked toward ending the counseling sessions, Jim and Laura were able to discuss the fear they both expressed earlier about being 40+. They felt they had lost control of the family in the eyes of the children because they were "over the hill".

At this point we took time to review some of the Bible characters like Abraham, Sarah, Moses, Anna, and others who were able to trust God despite their age. Then, Jim and Laura began to recall some Christian couples who were in their 50s, 60s, and 70s and continued to radiate quiet confidence and peace in their lives. Jim and Laura discovered that for these 50+ Christians living in the love, joy, and peace of the Lord is really significant and basic to marriage. As Jim and Laura live out their faith, the older Christian couples see Jim and Laura alive with a

Jim and Laura at 40+ now realize with thanksgiving that abundant life has only just begun!

spirit of excitement and anticipation each day. Eternal life has begun in reality for them here and now. Each day in Jesus is a new beginning! They are excited about dying to self to live abundantly. They understand bodily crucifixion is in process and are delighted to realize at 40+ they are also in the process of resurrection for eternity.

Jim and Laura have bonded together with their minds at ease about aging. They know that within the next eight years their children will be gone from the home to follow their careers in education and marriage. Love, joy, and peace in the Lord eventuates for those who worship God. The bible therefore became the focus for Jim and Laura's relationship. They covenanted together to concentrate on St. Paul's letter to the Ephesians by reading and living out in their marriage the godly wisdom contained in Chapters 4, 5, and 6. They have learned to be tenderhearted and forgiving of one another. The children have carefully observed these changes in Mom and Dad's relationship and this change has made them feel secure.

The humanism of the world failed to penetrate Jim and Laura's faith in Jesus for themselves and their children. Instead the Bible and the Holy Spirit provide them with an opportunity to make a choice to follow God (Luke 16:13). Jim and Laura at 40+ now realize with thanksgiving that abundant life has only just begun!

Application of and accountability for your faith is basic to being Christ-Centered.

Please refer to the next page and answer a few questions which may help you to bring your own situation into focus. God is faithful. By His grace you can seek His wisdom to help you with your life. Application of and accountability for your faith is basic to being Christ-Centered.[2]

---

2 Ibid

Reading about aging at 40+ is one thing, but applying what you read to your life is another. Jim and Laura represent many of us who claim to be Christians. This book encourages accountability in the Lord. These questions are designed to stimulate your thinking. Application and accountability for your life is based upon obedience to the Holy Spirit and the Word of God. It is exciting and dynamic to live and grow in grace and in the knowledge of our Lord and Savior Jesus Christ (2 Pet. 3:18b). You will enjoy self discovery in Jesus.

Are you like, Jim _____ Laura _____ pretending to be Christian but bound in chains by a busy humanistic world?
   ❑ Yes   ❑ No

Describe yourself in one word _____

Does your one-word description describe your life in Jesus at 40+ ?   ❑ Yes   ❑ No

Write one paragraph about who you are in Jesus.

Write a paragraph about why you are here in Jesus (what is the purpose of your life?).

Will you covenant that you will apply your faith and be accountable to God? ❑ Yes

Share this convenant with your prayer partner or prayer group.

Date _____.

CHAPTER 6

Aging is a Joyful Self-Discovery Paradigm[1]– *Get Involved With Living In Jesus and Change Your World for Jesus.* Life is a Great Adventure.

Do we deliberately deny God's will for our lives as we age by failing to live out the abundant life in Him?

"These things I have spoken to you, that in Me you may have peace. In this world you will have tribulation; but be of good cheer, I have overcome the world"

JOHN 16:33

In the previous chapter we discussed Jim, Laura, and their children. Most of us, like Jim and Laura as they arrived at the "over the hill" age of 40, are fearful of aging. Christians may not biblically consider our position, portion, precedence, or practice of aging in Jesus. Remember that our Lord and Savior Jesus is still alive and well 2000 years following His bodily death and resurrection.Therefore, I conclude from the bible that aging into eternal life is designed by God as our precedence, position, portion, and practice as Christians (John 3:16).

Jim 41, and Laura, 40, are at the threshold of love, joy, and peace in the Lord as they become Christ-centered in their individual and marital development. Being Christ-centered is biblical self-discovery of eternal significance. Jim and Laura are repre-

---

[1] "until we all reach unity in the faith and in the knowledge of the Son of God and become mature, attaining to the whole measure of the fullness of Christ." (Eph. 4:13). Mature *(helikia)* refers to matters relating to an individual's time of life.

sentative of contemporary society. Will they look forward in Jesus to 50, 60, 70, 80, 90, 100+ with a keen sense of joy and anticipation?

Abraham triumphed over age. Following Sarah's death Abraham lived to be 175. He lived in obedience to God. At 100 God gave Abraham a son named Isaac. Abraham never complained about his age or thought himself useless and not relevant. Abraham was open to God's leading and direction when God first spoke to him, "Then Abram believed in the Lord and He reckoned it to him as righteousness."

Are the cultural and environmental differences in Old Testament society and our contemporary world such that fear of aging has become our most malignant stressor? Once the negative worldly mind set of aging becomes the psychological tonus of life, even for a Christian, the forces of evil will hasten death. There is no hope for those who ignore or deny Jesus. Crucifixion of the body (physical death) is the end of life here on earth, but death should never be premature due to lack of biblical truth, faith and vision.

What is the difference between Old Testament society and our short-lived lives in this secular humanistic world? Could the answer be as simple as obedience to God? God called, Abraham obeyed! Age was no excuse for lack of obedience to God's plan for Abraham's life, nor for ours. (John 14:21,23).

Humanistic culture contributes heavily through the media to the misperception that age is to be dreaded.

Humanistic culture contributes heavily through the media to the misperception that age is to be dreaded. The media screams out of its own fear that aging should be avoided at all costs. The worldly, Hollywood and TV personalities employ face lifts, skin creams, and implants to preclude even the appearance of aging. In addition, the public is relentlessly bombarded by TV commercials and billboard advertising that exacerbates the paranoia of compulsive youthfulness.

Yet, culturally, genetic longevity is treasured! We send birthday cards to an older relative as a loving gesture. If the truth were known, the sender is delighted with the age of the older relative at 70, 80, 90, 100. Good family genes are predictors of longevity. Yet, there remains a heaviness of spirit about the reality of becoming old yourself and therefore useless and no longer relevant in the eyes of the world.

In the workplace there is even more brainwashing about age. Retirement is something to be worked for and anticipated with excitement until the time comes to retire. Thank God I have never had a retirement plan or worked for a company with a retirement plan, so that at 76 working full-time for the Lord has become a lifesaver instead of a curse. I can't afford to retire. What a blessing from God!

There is another fallacy involved with retirement from the work place. As an older person ages, despite his increasing skill due to long experience, this older person is often not considered for promotion and increased compensation. The 50+ person because of his age is often shunted aside despite demonstrated talents and abilities. This type of discrimmination is tragic.

An example of the way God works in the 50+ generation is Moses who was 80 when God gave him responsibility as a prophet and judge to lead the people of Israel out of Egypt. God equipped Moses to administer the welfare of more than one million people for a period of forty years. He took on this responsibility at 80 and continued until he was 120, still clear-eyed and vigorous. God did not discriminate against Moses because of his age.

But, today's society is so obsessed with youth, no one would consider a person of 80 years able to take on the level of responsibility Moses did. The present atmosphere of anxiety about aging represents Satanic humanism in a virulent form. Many older persons can make a significant contribution to those around them, just like my Mother at 95-98+ who, despite the loss of sight and hearing, was able with the love of Jesus in her heart to minister to her fellow residents in the nursing home. Many older people 60+ because of age and their own disability are more effective than other groups who lack the love for others.[2] Many younger people work in jobs that require service to older persons but they lack the love, patience, and compassion to enjoy their work and the preciousness of age which they may have the opportunity to experience themselves.

Some feel the elderly are unable able to contribute to others and consider euthanasia or suicide as the logical options for the elderly, invalid, or terminally-ill. Contrary to our society today no one suggested to Moses that he was a candidate for euthanasia—even at 120. Being aborted from society because you are sick and aged is psychological brainwashing in the Nazi tradition. It is Satanic! Emphasis should be on full utilization of all human resources and potential in Christ rather than eliminating God-ordained resources. All life is precious! Life is an environment that needs to be loved and protected. Life is valuable to self, others, and especially to God our Creator.[2]

Destruction of God-created life will eventually be accounted for to God by those who take life. This will include those who have presided over legislation and the legal system which is being used against the innocent. God created human life in His own image and likeness. Young people and adults who sanction abortion of unborn babies or allow the elderly to take their own lives, need to understand that Satan is the ultimate deceiver.

Suicide among the elderly is another method of elimination of valuable life and resources. Satan devised suicidal ideation because he desires mankind to be like him, an adversary of Almighty God:

---

[2] *Zoe* is "life intensive" and *bios* is "life extensive." *Bios* refers to the period or durations of life. *Zoe* is the nobler word, expressing as it continually does, all of the hightest and best which the saints possess in God (Trench., Syn.Sec.xxvii in Vine's Expository Dictionary of Biblical Words.) *Bios* is mentioned 11 times compared to *zoe* which is referred to 133 times in the New Testament.

"How you have fallen from heaven, O Lucifer, son of the morning! How you were cut down to the ground, you who weaken the nations. For you have said in your heart, I will ascend into heaven, I will exalt my throne above the stars of God, I will also sit on the mount of the congregation on the farthest sides of the north, I will ascend above the heights of the clouds, I will be like the most high, yet you shall be brought down to Sheol, to the lowest depths of the pit."

ISAIAH 14:12-15

Political correctness is the adversarial god of this world. Abortion at the inception of God-given life in the womb, euthanasia (abortion of the life of the elderly) and suicide (self-abortion) are all increasing as America follows Satan and his socialist humanistic minions. We, as a country, will have much to answer for. God said, "You shall not murder" (Ex. 20:13 NKJV). He will require an accounting. "What have you done? The voice of your brother's blood cries out to Me from the ground" (Gen. 4:10 NKJV).

Conversely, Christians as they age[3] should become more responsible and get involved with daily living in Jesus. One way is through political involvement. Most Christians deliberately avoid politics. We continue to pay the price for using the excuse that politics are dirty, and that Christians are above the political process. If we fail to pray and then vote we are totally responsible for the outcome of elections.

Jesus took responsibility! He made His stand in the public arena, in the temple, and in Pilate's court. We who claim to be Christians are responsible for Fabian socialism which is pervasive in our society today. Socialism invaded our democracy from the very beginning by giving preeminence to the rationalistic rule and law of man. Christians have assiduously avoided

---

[3] The "elder *(zaqen)*" in the Old Testament was recognized by the people for his gifts of leadership, wisdom and justice. He was set apart to administer justice, settle disputes, and guide the people of his charge. In a given city, the governing council was made up of the "elders," who were charged with the well-being of the town (Vines's Expository Dictionary of Biblical Words).

involvement in government and, therefore, are responsible for what has become religious persecution of Christians and the ungodly attack on biblical absolutes. Christians have allowed godless socialist humanism to takeover the local, state, and federal government. Shame on us who are 40+ and don't get involved in our country and world! I was one of those who was too busy to be informed, so I stood aside and permitted the godless to take over. At 76 I have the responsibility to sound the alarm and be counted for God's righteousness. It is never too late to be totally involved with living in the love, joy, and peace of Jesus. Life in Jesus is a great adventure! Older Christians do not realize that they can be a force for bringing about the Kingdom of God here on earth by the practice of their faith.

The solution to humanistic socialism is application of and accountability for our Christian faith. The Bible our authority, interpreted for us by God's Holy Spirit is as yet available to us. The Bible unequivocally states that we should follow Jesus. We have a clear choice. ". . . whosoever desires to come after Me, let him deny himself, and take up his cross, and follow Me. For whosoever desires to save his life will lose it, but whosoever loses his life for My sake and the gospel's will save it" (Mark 8:34,35). As we age scripture passages become infinitely more applicable and appealing. As we age the world loses its allure. The beautiful truth of the Bible becomes living reality. The Bible transitions time and has provided us with an encyclopedia of data that, for more than two thousand years, has never ever been refuted or proven untrue. Nevertheless, humanists who have failed to prove the bible untrue still refuse to acknowledge that Jesus is the Way, the Truth, and the Life (John 14:6). Application of our faith and accountability before God and man at 40+ is the certain way to reverse ungodly humanistic socialism. These are exciting times in which we live.

I challenge those of us who are 40+ and eager and willing to publish the Good News that Jesus saves (Ps. 96) to begin to devote their time to pray and take action in the political arena to effect change back to the Bible. The Bible was not written by man or woman, thereby subject to error, but by the Holy Spirit of God, therefore not subject to any error or change. The Bible is God's constitution for all mankind. Reading and studying the Bible is essential to enable Christians to communicate God's love and biblical absolutes. As we age, living out the Word of God is an exciting self-discovery paradigm. Getting involved with living in Jesus, life becomes a

> *Getting involved with living in Jesus, life becomes a great adventure.*

great adventure. Many Christians say they are too old, but if they believe the Bible no Christian is too old to serve the Living God and His Christ. Remember Moses?

Even Christians who claim to be young at heart have allowed themselves to be dis-spirited by the unremitting effects of a liberal humanistic society. The cry today is clean up the environment. I could not agree more. The godless, humanistic environment needs to be cleaned up and God expects and equips us to do it.

The enormous waste of human life and potential is undermining man's spirit with disastrous results. Often, Christians become filled with a sense of hopelessness praying for the Lord to return soon. Jesus will return when God is ready for that to happen. In the meantime, we who are 40+ should be about our Father's business with the love, joy, and peace of the Lord evident to those around us, not only in the church but in the world. Otherwise the Great Commission will never be fulfilled (Matt. 28:19,29; Acts 1:8), and God will hold us accountable. The humanistic odds against us are enormous, but we have God on our side! We have the final victory insured by Jesus Christ!

There has never been a better time in this world for us to live out faith by following the Lord. History continues to repeat itself. Read Isaiah, Jeremiah, Ezekiel, Habakkuk then try to deny that these books written millennia ago are not as current and relevant as tomorrow's newspaper. Read the New Testament and grow to appreciate the obstacles Jesus, Peter, John, Paul, and the women of the church had to face and endure.

My challenge is for those 40+ to disciple (Eph. 4:11-16) Christians worldwide to apply their faith and be biblically accountable. At 90, John, the beloved disciple, who was banished to the Isle of Patmos, totally rejected humanism when he wrote in and through the power of the Holy Spirit the Book of Revelation. John is the same man who in John 17: 10,19 quoted Jesus when he said, "we are His glory and we are sanctified by Him."

John, as a son of thunder in his youth, never thought he would be used by God in this most effective way at an advanced age. Not only did John write the Gospel and much later the Revelation but he finally left the Isle of Patmos and returned to Antioch, following the reign of Domitian, to live out his life in service to the Lord. Age was not a deterrent to John! He got involved in a great adventure. Today, we continue to study the Gospel of John, his epistles, and the Revelation two thousand years after they were written through the power of the Holy Spirit. These books and letters are beyond comparison in all the literature of men. John was challenged by the Holy Spirit to be faithful. He answered the challenge as a 90 year old author for Jesus Christ!

Often when a challenge is made, the one who issues the challenge falls far short of the expectations he has of others. In my case, I am unable to express to you even as I write these words the joy I feel that God would grant me life and health and strength to communicate the reality of His Word to you. As a Christian psychologist/advisor/consultant by education and training, I am able to perceive by the Holy Spirit the intent and purpose of the people with whom I am privileged to consult. Few if any of these precious hurting people even begin to understand what God has done by creating them in the image of His Son Jesus, nor do they realize the awesome potential each has in Jesus (Gen.1:27). If they did hurt would become excitement, hopelessness would be replaced by love, joy and peace.

The world would not be able to contain the books which could be written describing the plan God has formulated by Him for each of our lives before the beginning of time (Eph. 1:3-12). At 76, I am so privileged by God to share my enthusiasm about how life in Jesus is a great and peaceful adventure.

Instead of waiting with dread and apprehension for a physical condition to worsen or expect everyday that a life threatening illness will occur, why not look forward with keen anticipation and excitement for service in the army of the Lord as a Christian soldier. The limits that are beginning to be imposed on health care for the elderly who are very sick should spur us on to working out and keeping in top condition with good balance in our lives through prayer, Bible study, praise, adequate rest, good diet, exercise, and moderation in all things. What blessings.

Those 40+ who have debilitating disease may use their minds with enthusiasm to take on projects with biblical Christian purpose. Don't wait for someone to come along and set up a program for you. People of advanced age have endured wars, depression, famine, the bread lines, and other tragedies yet they have learned to be self-sufficient. These people can still function in service to the Lord. Many of our difficult experiences have uniquely prepared us for battles and victories ahead.

For example, what would happen to our educational system if we volunteered at school and invested ourselves in the lives of children of any race, creed, or color who have never been parented or grandparented? Jesus' love, if shared with these children and the teachers, would positively affect every school. School parents and grandparents are desperately needed for both students and teachers. We make false assumptions that the teachers and school staff have all the answers. That is not the case! School boards would enthusiastically support 40+ parenting and grandparenting which would be volunteer with no cost to the taxpayers. In the school system today it is a case of the blind leading the blind and then attempting without any experiential insight to teach our children and grandchildren. Christian seniors would definitely effect a change by giving love and time to the educators and students alike.

This could be a challenge we, as older Christians who are concerned parents and grandparents, can accept with great enthusiasm. We do not need to attack individuals. We need to love individuals in education with Jesus' love. Christians 40+ can make a significant difference in Jesus' name (John 15:12).

One such humanistic educational system is in the process of being changed by a 40+ lady who has used Jesus' love in her work as chairperson of a local school board. Her success is measured by her reelections as chairperson and the excellent achievements being accomplished in that school district. Her faithfulness to Jesus' teaching of agape love is evidenced by the love and respect of the community and the other school board members.

In addition to the impact 40+ people can make on the educational system there are many other opportunities available to affirm aging as a viable self-discovery paradigm and a time to help make a difference in our world for Christ. Life in Jesus is a great adventure, because God is sovereign over age and abilities. He will surprise you by equipping you to do things for Him that you never thought possible.

Christian men and women are equipped by the Holy Spirit to work effectively on a one-on-one basis over a period of time. Involvement in the education system with a larger social group may be delightful and interesting for some Christians. Other 40+ Christians may be more comfortable volunteering in business and industry as chaplains to the untold suffering that is reflected by the skyrocketing absenteeism in American industry. The military can always use Christian volunteers to help the chaplains with the floodtide of need in personal and family problems.

To illustrate a one-on-one relationship in a business setting: I met with Tom who had just turned 40. Tom looked at his life realistically. Over a period of years Tom felt the Lord leading him into a teaching, instruction ministry. His move from broadcasting and electronic communications was not a precipitous or inappropriate decision but one that was arrived at after much prayer.

Tom's previous career as a top executive in communications was marked by success after success based on his reputation as a hard-working, quiet, dynamic creative person. He did not, as many Christians do, leave a career filled with pain and failure to suddenly hear God calling him to the ministry. Tom had paid his dues and after much prayer yielded to the Holy Spirit to give his many and varied talents in service to God. I have never met anyone in ministry who prepared as well as this man to move from the commercial world into full-time service for the Lord. His primary interest was in the education and reconciliation of persons who had experienced divorce or separation, an area which is not recognized as a school course but in which Christian education is desperately needed.

This change took place when anyone else with Tom's talents and character would seek further advancement and compensation to assure his financial future. Instead, after diligently saving his earnings over and above his tithe and basic living expenses, Tom was able by God's grace to set aside adequate funds to carry out his well-thought-out plan for ministry. He prayed about being in the Lord first and then doing God's will for his life.

Tom's current plan is progressing efficiently and productively with vision and energy. He knows who he is in Jesus,[4] what he is doing and where he is going. The purpose for his life and

---

[4] Christ-Centered Personality Development, Dr. Robert Abarno, Copyright 1988, Second Edition, 1992, Third Edition 1994, Fourth Edition 1996.

how he is going to work his plan for Jesus are in motion by God's Holy Spirit. Here is a man who is 43 and moving productively in the Lord. He is not looking for retirement but for many active productive years in service to God and mankind. Tom told me that his life is getting better as he becomes more mature in the Lord, and his age is becoming an asset not a liability.

He prayed about being in the Lord first and then doing God's will for his life.

I have been privileged to participate as a Christian counselor in Tom's life over a period of seven years. During that period of time and continuing today he has passed through several stages of development. As an older advisor (as many of you who are older, wiser Christians can and should be) to a man who is ready to move to the next part of God's plan for his life, I felt a little like Moses leading God's man into the promised land where he would have many years of productive service for the Lord. Then, for Tom to guide another man to go through the process he and I had experienced.

Tom asked me to continue to consult with him in his potentially large national and international ministry. Moses felt inadequate for the responsibility of leading the Israelites out of Egypt. I feel as Moses did by being involved in counseling Tom. God has also privileged me to counsel 30 other men who labor in pastoral or lay ministries. These men range from 23 to 63. Being in Jesus at 76 enables me to counsel them from the Bible with confidence. Being 44 years in the Lord is helpful in my role with them. I know before God that I do not have a hook or personal agenda to promote with these men. There is great joy in helping men to see their potential in Jesus.

Aging has been a self-discovery paradigm for my life. My involvement living in the love, joy, and peace of Jesus is fulfilling and a great adventure. Therefore I continue to relate to Moses as a biblical model for self-discovery and great adventure. My prayer is to benefit from my age like Moses, and to be a humble friend of God.

Moses had three specific periods of 40 years each during his span of life here on earth before God took him at 120 when Moses was still clear-eyed and vigorous. Life for Moses consisted of three very different 40 year careers. First, he was a prince in the house of Pharaoh. Next, a herdsman in the back of the desert. Then, God made Moses a prophet and judge of Israel. The last two 40 year stages of Moses' career were far more exciting than the first 40 years of his life.

Moses had the awesome experience of being in the presence of God on the mountain top for forty days. God spoke to Moses a number of times. Moses was described as a friend of God. Later Moses also appeared with the Lord on the Mount of Transfiguration. Few fiction writers would be able to write a story or script a play which included such awesome drama. Anything that man has ever experienced pales into insignificance when compared to Moses' life as recorded in the Bible. Think of how God intervened when Moses was 40+ and how that was only the beginning of his usefulness to God. The three stages of Moses' life were exciting and dynamic but are only a preview of Moses' eternal life in the presence of the Lord God Almighty.

Do we deliberately deny God's will for our lives by failing to die to self and live the abundant life in Him at 40, 50, 60, 70, 80, 90, 100+? Self-discovery of God's plan for our lives (Eph. 1:3-12) revealed to us by the Holy Spirit is the most exciting, interesting challenge in life.

> As it is written, "Eye has not seen, nor ear heard, neither have entered into the heart of man, the things which God has prepared for those who love Him."
>
> 1 CORINTHIANS 2:9

Live out with great enthusiasm what God has in store for you in Jesus Christ. At 40+ we can live the abundant life in

Jesus in exciting and fulfilling ways. Jesus did not say "I have come to give you life and give it to you abundantly until you are 40." There is no time limit on the abundant life in Jesus. Abundant life in Jesus is eternal! At 40, 50, 60, 70, 80, 90, 100+ we have only just begun!

Praise God from whom all blessings flow! As I enjoy my crucifixion and as I enter into the resurrection process what I have written becomes very real. Daily I examine where I am with the Lord. Without fear I joyfully acknowledge my age. Daily intimacy with Jesus may precede or follow my daily devotions. I have discovered that what I previously perceived as physical, emotional, or spiritual impediments was, upon prayer and meditation, something God allowed. More importantly I discovered His purpose was to teach me about His intimate involvement with my life—my crucifixion and resurrection.

This learning and discovery paradigm is exciting! I am able to write about my own crucifixion and resurrection process because I am engaging in it now. Up until this writing I was not prepared to articulate my understanding of God's agape love and the growing intimacy (resurrection) I have with Him. I look forward to additional time in the future to share with others what God is teaching me. Of one thing I am certain. Based upon biblical intimacy with Jesus there is peace within my soul which passes all understanding. I agape and praise God from whom all blessings flow.

Aging is the time when we look forward to relaxing without stress. Have you ever considered that aging in faith in Jesus Christ is the relaxing wisdom of the gospel?

From a thankful heart I invite you to join with me in a joyful self-discovery paradigm which is a great adventure in the love, joy, and peace of the Lord. Get involved in life and change your world through Jesus. Life in Him has only just begun!

Many of us have heard people say, "Old too soon, too late smart." That statement and philosophy is not biblical. Read on in the next chapter and see how faith and wisdom are related. Aging is the time when we look forward to relaxing without stress. Have you ever con-

Older in Jesus is not better it is best!

sidered that aging in faith in Jesus Christ is the relaxing wisdom of the gospel? Older in Jesus is not better it is best!

Is it really possible for God to use me at my age?

❏ Yes   ❏ No

If not, why not? Explain with biblical references your reasons for being unable to be used by God.

Pray and ask God to reveal to you who you are in Jesus. Then write one paragraph about the potential (gifts, talents, and abilities) you have in Jesus to serve God in your daily life.

Do you believe your life will become filled with the love, joy, and peace of the Lord as you grow older in Jesus?

❏ Yes   ❏ No

Be specific and describe in writing how God is evident to you. Then share your self discovery with others and encourage them to be in Jesus in order to do His will for their lives. You cannot share that aging in Jesus is best unless you know it is joyfully manifest in your own life in Him.

CHAPTER 7

Faith is the Relaxing Wisdom of the Gospel (Good News)[1]

"What does it profit, my brethren, if someone says he has faith but does not have works? Can faith save Him?

JAMES 2:14

I will show you my faith by my works.

JAMES 2:18

If you are wise, live a life of steady goodness, so that only good deeds will pour forth... But the wisdom that comes from heaven is first of all pure and full of quiet gentleness.

JAMES 3:13.17

And the child grew and became strong in spirit, filled with wisdom, and the grace of God was upon Him.

LUKE 2:40

Jesus increased in wisdom, stature and favor with God and men.

LUKE 2:40

Although I have heard some children described as bright, intelligent, sharp, quick, responsive, or perceptive, I cannot ever recall hearing someone in early or later childhood, a teenager, or a young adult described as wise except for Jesus. He is wisdom personified. Wisdom has been traditionally associated with or accorded to the elderly by God (Ps.92).

Is faith in God the beginning of wisdom? Is Jesus a gift to humanity as the fullest expression of God's wisdom? Is faith in

---

[1] "And that from childhood you have known the sacred writings which are able to give you the wisdom that leads to salvation through faith which is in Christ Jesus" (2 Tim. 3:15).

God relaxing wisdom? I find it delightful to meditate on these questions knowing that God loves us and wants us to understand His love in our relationship with Him.

Faith is the relaxing wisdom of the Gospel. The Gospel is the good news from God by His infinite mercy and grace to all of humanity. "Wisdom gives:

A long, good life
Riches
Honor
Pleasure
Peace

Wisdom is a tree of life to those who eat her fruit; happy is the man who keeps on using it.
PROVERBS 1:16-18

We can rest in the knowledge that through Jesus we have eternal life by faith which is relaxing wisdom from God. The relaxing wisdom of faith should be especially significant to those who are 40, 50, 60, 70, 80, 90, and 100+. Age at 40-100+ is a blessed time to fully appropriate and trust God's wisdom in holy living without stress here and now and for all time and eternity.

The Bible states correctly that wisdom comes from God alone.[2] The Bible contains many references to wisdom:

Happy is the man who finds wisdom and the man who gains understanding for her proceeds are better than the profits of silver, and her gain more than fine gold. Wisdom is more precious than rubies and in all things you may desire cannot compare with wisdom. Length of days is in her right hand and in her left hand, riches and honor. Her ways are ways of pleasantness and in all her paths are peace. Wisdom is a tree of life (no limits on age are

---

[2]   "that the God of our Lord Jesus Christ, the Father of glory, may give to you a spirit of wisdom and of revelation in the knowledge of Him" (Eph. 1:17).

mentioned) *to those who take hold of it. Happy are all who retain it.*

P R O V E R B S   3 : 1 3 - 1 8

In the Bible, wisdom is described through the Hebrew "hocham," the Greek "sophos" meaning learned, prudent, or clever, *to be (a verb form)* wise or act wisely. Biblical wisdom is "the Lord by wisdom founded the earth, by His understanding, He established the heavens, by His knowledge the depths were broken and the clouds dropped down the dew" (Prov. 3:19, 20). *To be* wise is *to be* godly.

Jesus is the personification of wisdom. "...you are in Christ Jesus, who became for us wisdom from God" (1 Cor. 1:30). Personal salvation in Jesus is the relaxing wisdom of faith. What is more wise and relaxing than by faith to trust implicitly in Jesus? (Ps. 31:1)

As Christians grow older, we should be far more relaxed than others, not more stressed by our age.[3] For myself, I have learned as I age that wisdom is faith in Jesus in daily life, not sitting around in self- pity or depression waiting to die. We have the promise of eternal life through the death and bodily resurrection of Jesus. Either we Christians believe in eternal life or we do not. If we believe, we must refuse to be immobilized by preoccupation with death. Age is the most beautiful and vital stage in God's plan for us as we accept and appreciate His love and grace with great dignity. His peace becomes our peace and the quietness of our spirit becomes a dynamic witness to others. His wisdom is our wisdom reflected by us as contentment in Him.

Therefore aging, the gradual crucifixion of our flesh is not a fearful process. Although crucifixion in the form of aging is inevitable due to original sin, we can rejoice in God's wonderful provision for us and look forward in Jesus with delight because our future is assured! "And I give them eternal life, and they shall never perish; neither shall anyone snatch them out of my

---

[3] "I thought age should speak, and increased years should teach wisdom" (Job 32:7).

hand" (John 10:28).

Christians will spend eternity with God. He will retain for us our God-given individual personality in a heavenly body which will never be sick or die. Our identity, who we are is assured for eternity.

Therefore in Jesus, we can accept the process of aging with calmness, equanimity, love, joy, and peace in the Lord. The relaxing wisdom of faith is the discovery paradigm of what the Gospel means [4], the Good News that God is, therefore in Jesus, I am.[5] Christians who have faith in Jesus may be totally unaware that biblical faith is relaxing wisdom. Enjoy!

> *The Good News that God is, therefore in Jesus, I am.*

God's Word is our written assurance that aging (preparation for heaven) can be the best time of our lives. During our aging process God is preparing a new body for each of us in heaven (2 Cor. 5). We will in due course give up our human body for this perfect heavenly body. Our heavenly body will not be sick, diseased, or burdensome, but absolutely delightful!

Our individual uniqueness, our personality/soul (mind, will, and emotions) will inhabit our heavenly body. We will be identified in heaven by our individual personality as each of us is known by our individual personality here in this world. Our daily prayer in Jesus' name should be that our individual personality will be Christ-centered here and now during our crucifixion and in our resurrection for eternity.

Faithful St. Paul with wisdom from the Holy Spirit, tells us the biblical order of our resurrection, dying to live abundantly forever.

> *But now Christ is risen from the dead, and has become the first fruits of those who have fallen asleep. For since by*

---

[4] "Yet we do speak wisdom among those who are mature; a wisdom, however, not of this age, nor of the rulers of this age, who are passing away" (1 Cor. 2:6).

[5] Christ-Centered Personality Development, Dr. Robert Abarno, Copyright 1988, Second Edition 1992, Third Edition 1994, Fourth Edition 1996. All rights reserved.

man came death, by man also came the resurrection of the
dead. For as in Adam all die, even so in Christ all shall be
made alive.

1 CORINTHIANS 15:20-22

Isn't it exciting to know and understand that "we shall be made alive". We shall enjoy the blessings of our bodily crucifixion, yes blessings superceding what by the world's standards is a time of fear, pain and sorrow. Then we shall enjoy our forthcoming heavenly body and soul resurrection. I am beginning to experience what I am writing. There is a transition contained in these two processes which I am barely able to describe. I have a compelling desire to share the beauty and holiness of God's provision for me. because I am now certain that my faith is the relaxing wisdom of the Gospel (Good News) of Jesus Christ (John 3:16).

I perceive these two processes going on simultaneously within me and they are close and very real. The first is the process of my physical body being crucified, deteriorating slowly day by day yet in my case without significant pain or disease. Conversely, Jesus' crucifixion was painful, humiliating, and it took a relatively short time for death to occur. My crucifixion time has been much longer, without much pain and a beautiful time for praise, worship and thanksgiving. I can only report what I have experienced thus far in my crucifixion process and contrary to what I thought would be a painful, fearsome process I am surprised by contentment and joy.

In addition to my personal salvation in which I rejoice even more as I age, I ask myself what other implications does Jesus' sacrificial death and resurrection have for me? Is it just possible that my personal crucifixion, the demise of my physical body and presence here on earth, has some eternal significance? Does sharing this process by God's grace help to allay the fear, boredom, anger, loneliness and trepidation usually associated with aging and dying? If so, praise God!

On the cross Jesus was not preoccupied by the suffering of his physical body. Despite the excruciating painful process of bodily crucifixion, Jesus' concentration was focused on others. For example, on the sinner who was crucified with Him. One convicted criminal confessed his guilt and then professed his faith in Jesus. Despite His own pain and suffering Jesus forgave this man. Then, Jesus even forgave those who crucified Him. Jesus was faithful and obedient to God and thus because of His faith became the model for the relaxing wisdom of the Gospel in our crucifixion process.

> *"I will love him and manifest (reveal) Myself to him." (John 14:21 NKJV)*

The benefit of my crucifixion process is that aging and dying are the greatest opportunities I have ever had in my life to rejoice in my Lord and Savior Jesus Christ. Jesus demonstrated for me that He is the Way, the Truth, and the Life (John 14:6). His own suffering meant little to Jesus when compared to being obedient to His Father's will. Jesus said, "He who has My commandments and keeps them, it is he who loves Me. And he who loves Me will be loved by My Father, and I will love him and manifest (reveal) Myself to him" (John 14:21 NKJV).

The reality for me of the crucifixion process is the biblical intimacy developed in my life through the joy of willing obedience to follow Jesus so that, "they may have My joy fulfilled in themselves" (John 17:13b) because, "they are not of the world as I am not of the world" (John 17:16).

Therefore, my preparation time (aging) for leaving the world is not a time of sadness, fear, dread, or apprehension but a time of joy with keen anticipation for what God has guaranteed for me for eternity.

At the risk of being misunderstood I do not have any inclination to hurry up the process of bodily crucifixion. I am not impatient to die. Each day however I do experience with much thanksgiving the love, joy, and peace of the Lord which rests solely upon my faith in Jesus—the relaxing wisdom of the Gospel (Good News).

The good news to which I refer is another process taking place concurrent with bodily crucifixion. I identify the second process as my sanctification which is the beginning of my resurrection! Part of my sanctification is the joy I experience in writing this book to reach out to others to share my faith in Jesus. That is relaxing wisdom which is active and fulfilling, not passive.

I am unable to count the hours I have devoted to writing this book, meditating, praying, enjoying, and looking to the Lord Jesus for direction. Of one

> *$\mathcal{I}$ speak here of peace which is my position and practice of liberty in Christ which I will address later in Chapter 9.*

thing I am certain. Writing from the heart by His Holy Spirit has been the most rewarding growth experience I have ever had. I would not want to redeem these precious hours to be used in any other way! I speak here of peace which is my position and practice of liberty in Christ which I will address later in Chapter 9.

I count it a privilege from God to encourage Christians to "lighten up and be real!" If God's Holy Spirit works in and through me in the process of sanctification so that I bear the fruit of love, joy, peace, patience, gentleness, goodness, faithfulness, meekness, and self-control then all other Christians can also be similarly blessed. Bearing sanctified fruit is the result of my being in Jesus. Some of the things God has enabled me to do are a constant source of peace to me. My being in Jesus is eternally secure. My self discovery paradigm at 76 is to observe objectively, without any panic, my bodily functions begin to decrease and, at the same time, rejoice as my Christ-centered personality/soul (mind, will, and emotions) begin to increase.

As I age I am no longer bound by the constraints of this socialist, humanistic world. I am absolutely convinced that God has the best plan for me. I daily pass, by way of bodily crucifixion and the falling away of worldly constraints, to life eternal

with my soul and spirit intact. I am looking forward with anticipation to my heavenly body (2 Cor. 5:17) which will not get sick,
require constant attention, suffer in pain, or die!

Rarely as I look forward to the perfect state of being in
heaven with Jesus does my faith waver. When this occurs I
have to laugh because I realize I am testing my faith. About six
months ago, a large company advertised an annuity plan for
elderly persons who may not have enough insurance to pay for
the cost of nursing home care should that be required. I mailed
back a request for more information. Several weeks passed, and
then I received a telephone call from a saleslady requesting an
appointment. My wife and I agreed on a date and time for the
appointment.

As this efficient, articulate, pleasant sales representative
made her presentation I deliberately allowed myself to think
about the implications of her presentation. Her primary purpose
was to provide a plan to help bear the cost of residence in a
nursing home if I became debilitated and too much of a burden
for my wife. I understood the factual part of the presentation. I
was in shock when I realized that this presentation was for me!
The sales representative and my wife were actually discussing
my future incapacitating illness(es) not someone else's.

Reality set in during the time we spent with this lady. I was
the object of this meeting. The annuity which would be built up
to pay for the expense of nursing home care was now secondary. I had, without much thought or feeling but constrained
by others to initiate preparation for being set aside, becoming
debilitated, unable to take care of myself. This is me we were
discussing not some relative or friend.

I pointed out in Chapter 1 that my mother had become a
resident in a nursing home and how God used her in service to
him when she was 95-98+. Now I am approaching my turn if
such care becomes necessary. Suddenly all I have written came
into perspective for me! It is one thing to write objectively if you
are not personally involved but it is quite another to be subjec-

tively involved. Reality reminds me that this discussion is up close and personal.

My mother did very well serving God in the nursing home even though she had been adamant about not wanting to end up there. Her closest friend had a terrible experience in a nursing home, so Mother denied even to the day she died that she was a resident in a nursing home, preferring to persuade herself that she was in a medical facility.

Enter faith, the relaxing wisdom of the Gospel. God protected and occupied Mother in service to Him to the last day of her life. My mother's ability to function with the love, joy, and peace of the Lord without fear, distress or concern about her environment enabled me to begin to examine my faith as the relaxing wisdom of God in His plan for my crucifixion and resurrection. Mother essentially had completed her transition in Jesus although she was still alive she was in reality already in the resurrection process. She was oriented to and conversive with her environment but had already moved ahead with the Lord as her constant companion. All other things were behind her and the peace in her soul was obvious.

My time is approaching. Is my faith the relaxing wisdom of the Gospel? I look forward with anticipation and joy to experience this transition. In fact, after having written about crucifixion and resurrection I realize I am well into these transitions and yet I enjoy a deep sense of peace and well being in Jesus. I do not dwell on my departure. I am more interested in the events which cause me to reflect on what is happening and the almost child like curiosity I have about crucifixion and resurrection experiences.

With the possibility of incapacitating illness ahead, is the love, joy, and peace of the Lord just something to write about or something to live out on a daily basis? Am I prepared to rely on Jesus with peace and joy in whatever situation I find myself? As I find my way through my occasional self testing experiences I remember the times I walked through some of these experiences with older relatives and older friends assuring them without personal experience of the benign nature of the stages of dying and death. I was at those times an expert on something I had not experienced nor did I feel that I was even close to dying.

Another interesting and amusing experience I have recently been involved in was a response card I mailed to a funeral home. My intent was to sit down with someone in my office and objectively discuss a procedure for handling the remains of my bodily crucifixion. My purpose was to relieve my wife of any burden involved in the funeral home and burial arrangements.

A bright young man in his early 30s answered my request and appeared at my office one day. As this young man whose name was David outlined the various plans available following my demise, I mentally absented myself during his presentation to think about what was happening. We were discussing me, addressing my death and burial. While this young man was speaking, I asked myself, is this part of crucifixion in the love, joy, and peace of the Lord ? My humanness— my vulnerability— was beginning to surface.

My faith in Jesus momentarily receded into the background of my mind and heart. When I realized this, I laughed out loud. My laughter startled this proper and serious young man who was trying to do his job of persuading me about the efficacy of making funeral plans ahead of time. I know I embarrassed him so I attempted to explain to him as best I could my response to the situation in which I found myself. I think that he understood when I told him the reason I laughed was because my faith was in question. He was only 30, and had some difficulty in understanding my situation because dying was something he dealt with objectively not subjectively.

I was in the process of writing this book in which I define faith as the relaxing wisdom of the Gospel (Good News). Therefore, if I am overwhelmed, fearful, or anxious about my bodily crucifixion, I am of all people most miserable. In fact, I am a liar. I am utilizing the Word of God for my own illusory purpose. Do I really believe what I am writing? These thoughts sobered me as David continued his presentation.

After David left my office I had a terrible sinking feeling of dread and apprehension as if something was impending that I had never experienced before. I felt and thought my life was in jeopardy. It seemed as though death was only a breath away, and that my life was over. This feeling, and the heaviness of spirit persisted for several minutes. I was virtually immobilized. My faith had ebbed, then flowed back and I was able to relax. I prayed to God in Jesus' name that if I had sinned unknowingly against Him He would forgive me. My dispirited feelings and thoughts passed, but I knew I was deeply humbled before God as though I had been on holy ground and He granted insight to share with others.

The Holy Spirit enabled me to understand that bodily crucifixion is temporary and transient. Faith is the relaxing wisdom of the gospel, the Good News (John 3:16) of eternal life. I know that faith in Jesus is my acknowledgment and submission to the biblical order for my crucifixion and resurrection.

I know it is not pleasing to Satan to exhort Christians who are 40+ to live their faith daily in the love, joy, and peace of the Lord. 40+ is a time[6] of beginnings not the humanistic time of being "over the hill." Attacking the bastions of hell in Jesus' name may have been the reason for personal discomfort in discussing my death with David. By the power of the Holy Spirit I am able to share with others my impending death in terms of here and now. I have approached Christians and those who are yet to come to Christ with the "inner satisfaction"[7] of becoming, by obedience to the Word of God, the image and likeness of His Son (Gen. 1:26,27,31).

I share biblical truth by learning to encapsulate each day with prayer. As I awaken in the morning, my prayer for God's

---

[6] **T i m e** – the intimate moment eternal, Christ-Centered Personality Development, Copyright 1988, Fourth Edition 1996.

[7] Unpublished siliioquy. Robert D. Gorham, Rocky Mount, NC 1995.

protection gives me great comfort. I devote my day to Him. As I close my eyes at night, I thank and praise the Lord. Daily devotion of my life to Jesus is like being with my best friend who wants the best for me every moment of the day and night.

I am quite surprised by what takes place each day in my walk with Jesus. I am not yet completely detached from the hysteria and concerns of the world. They surround me on every side. However, the humanistic world in which I live has been assaulted and penetrated by the relaxing wisdom of faith in the name and shed blood of Jesus our Lord and Savior.

I am dying to live abundantly in the love, joy and peace of the Lord. Praise God!

In the early morning hours, it is very quiet, so much so that I can hear the quiet. As I wake up I am delighted that I have the opportunity to listen quietly to Jesus within my being and know He is available anytime. I have to guard against the "gimmes and wants" but once I realize that is what I am doing, I reject them and enjoy the fellowship of His Holy Spirit. The gentleness, love, and comfort of the Holy Spirit is full of peace. After a peaceable conversation, I drift back to sleep with the blessed assurance that I am in sync with my Lord and Holy Comforter.

Under the watch care and protection of Jesus, "I can rejoice evermore, pray without ceasing, and in everything gives thanks for this is the will of God in Christ Jesus for you (and me)" (1 Thess. 5:16-18). It has taken me many years in the Lord to begin to understand and appropriate the fact that my faith in Jesus as Lord and Savior is the relaxing wisdom of the Gospel. (God's Good News to us is Jesus!) Knowing this basic fact of life, I—my being, my soul (mind, will, and emotions)—rejoice as each day brings me closer to my resurrected eternal life! I am dying to live abundantly in the love, joy and peace of the Lord. This is the relaxing wisdom of the Gospel. Praise God!

APPLICATION & ACCOUNTABILITY

Can you relate to faith as the relaxing wisdom of the Gospel? ❏ Yes   ❏ No

If you can, try to write a few words or lines about your personal faith being relaxing because of your personal faith in Jesus. Try to include a few bible verses which helps you confirm your faith as relaxing wisdom such as Prov.4:5-9.

Do you encapsulate your daily life with prayer for wisdom? ❏ Yes   ❏ No

If you have not sought God's direction, leading, protection, and watch care in prayer for godly wisdom how well have you been functioning ?   0 - 10 _____

Do you feel secure in your faith in Jesus and thereby in His love?   0 - 10 _____

Can you define your faith from scripture in your own words? It might be interesting for you to take the time to exegete your faith from Hebrews 11. Searching the scriptures for God's truth for your life provides great comfort and insight to live in the love, joy, and peace of the Lord.

Do you know that "gospel" means the "good news" that Jesus saves? Does this good news give you comfort, security, and inner peace?   0 - 10 _____

At 40+ are you beginning to think, speak, and live biblically for eternity? ❏ Yes   ❏ No

Take time to meditate and pray about these questions. They are not a quiz but are prayerfully designed for practical application and accountability in your life which is so precious to God.

RELAXING WISDOM

**THE GOSPEL
(GOOD NEWS)**

CHAPTER 8

≋

Being a Love Letter from God, is to Rejoice Evermore, Which is God's Will for Each Person's Life in Jesus

I have included this biblical concept in *Christ-Centered Personality Development.*[1] I ask CCPD readers and those readers who are also CCPD students to write a love letter from themselves to God, thanking Him, that they are a love letter from Him to a sick and dying world. An individual commitment to Jesus Christ as Lord and Savior places each of us in a position by faith to become a living love letter to those who are lost (Matt. 28:19, 20). But we can only write this epistle if we are living out our faith with integrity and love. Application of and accountability for our faith in Jesus transforms us to become a living love letter especially at 40+ to a sick and dying world and thus fulfill the Great Commission (Matt. 28:19, 20). Do not ever think or feel or allow someone to persuade you that God does not have a wonderful purpose for your life.

As we become sanctified by Him (John 17:19), our faith in Jesus eventuates into peaceable relaxing wisdom similar to Jesus' faith in God the Father (Prov. 3:1-8, 13-26 TLB). Our relaxing wisdom of faith prompts us to be in Jesus in order to do His good works (James 2:17-18). God's love letter to us is Jesus, the Living Word, the Bible:

The Living Word became flesh and dwelt among us.

JOHN 1:14

---

[1] Christ-Centered Personality Development, Dr. Robert Abarno, Copyright 1988, Second Edition 1992, Third Edition 1994, Fourth Edition 1996. All rights reserved.

To Christians, Jesus Christ is God's glory!

Jesus said, 'They are my glory.

JOHN 17:10

Glory, in the above verse, is synonymous with the word reputation[2]. Christians, who are living love letters to God and from Him to a sick and dying world, actually become His reputation here on earth. We are His living testimonies to those who are hurting and searching for the love, joy, and peace of the Lord Jesus. The Holy Spirit wrote the Bible through men of God. As personal love letters from God to a sick and dying world we become the only Bible some people will ever read. We are privileged to follow the model of who Jesus is—God's love letter to us. Think about the implications of a love letter written or received. There is a significant impact both on the writer and the recipient. When I am a love letter from God to someone I become observable by that person not only for how I look but by how I live out Jesus Christ.

For seven years I served in a ministry which was directed toward counseling pastors and other leaders in the church. I saw more despair, disarray, and despondency in those church leaders than I ever did with the people I counseled in private practice. The church leaders did not seem to have the love, joy, and peace of the Lord. The lack of joy was especially significant. Pastors and leaders are looked up to as models of steadfastness, especially in their faith. Instead of being models of Jesus, what the body of believers and the world frequently observe in their leaders is busy preoccupation. A pastor's schedule is unremitting and always paramount often to the exclusion of personal, family and pastoral needs.

I have included on page 108 in this book a time schedule,

Time = the intimate moment eternal.

---

2   Unshared Love Forum Series, Bob Mumford, Raleigh, NC, 1994, 1995.

entitled, "A Christian's Stewardship of T I M E (The Intimate Moment Eternal). How Do I Spend God's Gift of Time Each Week?"[3] There are 168 (24 x 7) hours in a week. It is relatively easy to tithe 10% of your income to God, but somewhat more difficult to tithe 10% of 168 hours (approximately 17 hours a week) to the Lord. God lovingly grants us 168 hours x 60 minutes x 60 seconds which equal 60,480 moments each week. It is important for Christians to recognize and joyfully devote 10% of this time to be faithful to God in praise, worship, adoration, and prayer.

I gave the CCPD Time Schedule to 20 pastors to complete as a CCPD class assignment. With the exception of one pastor's wife who completed and returned the Time Schedule, none of the pastors did so. I wondered why the pastors did not complete the assignment. It is easy to condemn them, yet we all seem to have the same problem with busyness, so much so that we neglect God. Ten percent of our time devoted to God is not legalism. In daily prayer, worship, praise, adoration, and service this time can be pure joy!

How can pastors, elders, leaders, and all Christians be love letters from God to their families, to the church, and to the world if they're so busy? My purpose in focusing on time tithing is to ask those who are 40+ not to become burdened with schedule. As a result of inordinate busyness and preoccupation with schedule there is no time tithing. We who are in Jesus should tithe our time to rejoice evermore, pray without ceasing and in everything give thanks to God.

As I age t i m e becomes even more the intimate moment eternal. Every time I take a breath I rejoice and thank God for the air I breathe and the lungs with which to breathe. Sounds simple, yet breathing is absolutely essential to life. I have become so attuned to my total dependency upon God for the basic functions of life, i.e., like the beat of my heart, is a preeminent

---

[3] Ibid, 1.

How do I spend God's gift of time each week?* 2 CHRONICLES 7:14-16

A CHRISTIAN'S STEWARDSHIP OF TIME (THE INTIMATE MOMENT ETERNAL)

There are 168 hours in a week.* We as Christians must tithe our time as well as our other resources. As you continue to use this time schedule and your prayer list, please note the increasing amount of time you have for the Lord and for the essentials of living. Also note how much more you are able to accomplish in your daily life when you tithe your time to the Lord first. (PS. 39:4,5; PS. 89:47; PS. 90:12; LUKE 12:16-23; EPH. 5:15-17 KJV)

* A 10% tithe for one week (168 hours in a week) equals 17 hours with the Lord and in His service.

**Emotional Acting and Reacting (Personal Emotional Pollution) i.e., confusion, jealousy, anger, fear, anxiety, shame/guilt, sadness/sorrow, disgust/revulsion, emptiness/aloneness.

©1988 Dr. Robert Abarno. Second Ed. 1992, Third Ed. 1994, Fourth Ed. 1996, CCPD.

108

Personal Time Table (Accountability) – Sanctification in Process

TIME SPENT PER WEEK	DATE:	1 MO.	3 MO.	6 MO.	9 MO.	1 YR.	2 YRS.	5 YRS.
Prayer, Meditation & Bible Study								
Personal/Prayer Partner Development								
Family Devotions								
Church/Small Group/Sunday School								
Ministry/Service								
TV Viewing								
Educational (Public TV)								
Recreational (Sports)								
Escape (TV Movies, Sit-Comedies)								
Eating								
Sleeping								
Working/Education/Career								
Exercise								
Relational Development								
Marriage (communication/spouse)								
Children, Family Time								
Friends								
Recreation								
Sports								
Hobbies								
Other Interests								
Telephone								
**EAR (PEP)								
Other								
TOTAL								

reason to rejoice evermore. My joy in living for Jesus becomes an opportunity for automatic praise, worship, thanksgiving, and adoration. To express this joy, I have deliberately chosen to become a love letter from God to a sick and dying world.

Being a love letter from God is no easy task for me a sinner saved by God's agape love and grace. Nevertheless being a love letter has now become the joyful reality of my life. Being representative of His Glory—by being His reputation here on earth—has given real purpose for my life. I have always felt productive when I have been able to help others to come to know the

> *Jesus is a love letter from God to me. I read the Bible for many years without ever having realized the Bible is His love letter to me.*

Lord Jesus. I am able at 76 to understand the biblical reality of Jesus being the Living Word of God. Jesus is a love letter from God to me. I read the Bible for many years without ever having realized the Bible is His love letter to me. I realize I now live in biblical intimacy with God. Words fail me to describe what I know and feel as I learn more about Him (John 17:3).

The Holy Spirit has led me into being Christ-centered in who I am and why I am here. During my crucifixion process I have come to understand the purpose of my life in Jesus.

If we take tithing time to meditate about it we can rejoice in Jesus , without the constraints of time or schedule to limit our joy. Time with Jesus are the intimate moments eternal in which life has only just begun. At 40+ we should not begin to concentrate on our aches and pains. Instead we should enjoy as His children the promises of the Living Word which proclaim:

> *Eye has not seen, nor ear heard, nor have entered into the heart of man the things that God has prepared for those who love Him.*
>
> 1 CORINTHIANS 2:9

Now we have received, not the spirit of the world, but the Spirit who is from God, that we might know the things that have been freely given us by God. These things we also speak not in words which man's wisdom teaches but what the Holy Spirit teaches, comparing spiritual things with spiritual. But the natural man does not receive the things of the Spirit of God, for they are foolishness to him; nor can he know them, because they are spiritually discerned

1 CORINTHIANS 2:12-14

As I write this book my heart rejoices in God's goodness, grace, and mercy. I discern the leading of the Holy Spirit as I record the scriptures He has given me to share with you, the reader. As I write this love letter to Him and from Him to you, my hearts' desire is to publish the Good News of the Gospel of Jesus on a personal level as biblical intimacy. Most men and

God is, therefore, in Jesus Christ I am.

even some women are reluctant to consider being intimate. Freedom from that bondage is being biblically intimate for God's honor and glory.

My personality, my soul, my uniqueness testifies that only God can give joy evermore! God has given each of us in Jesus a uniqueness which as it is given expression in our lives, enables us to become a beautifully written living epistle to others of His love and grace.

God has uniquely designed me to be an encourager, an exhorter. My ability to rejoice evermore develops as I encourage others to believe in their heart and say, "God is, therefore, in Jesus Christ I am."

I rejoice because:

- For me, biblical truth is reality. Biblical intimacy is abundant life now and for eternity!

- My faith is the relaxing wisdom that assures me that dying (crucifixion) is living abundantly (resurrection)! Both of these processes are in motion simultaneously.

- For me, to rejoice evermore is the triumph of Christianity over socialistic humanism.
- I am able to apply and be accountable for my faith.
- For me, like Abraham, Sarah, Moses, Caleb, Anna, John, and my mother before me, age is no barrier.
- Unlike my father I do not have to be silent and burdened with aloneness all of my life.
- I have biblical intimacy, maturity and relevance in my life.
- I am not deterred by aging. I enjoy my age because of Jesus!
- Aging has been and still is the most wonderful time of my life.
- As I age under the guidance of the Holy Spirit I am dealing with the problem of anger and am, by God's grace, gaining the victory.
- I am fully aware that without Jesus, it is boring, boring, boring to grow old!
- I rejoice that in Jesus anyone under 40 and anyone approaching 40 are also able to enjoy, relax, and develop spiritually in the aging process.
- Aging is wonderful! Aging is a discovery paradigm! A new and abundant life has begun!
- The Holy Spirit has enabled me to live my life by faith which is truly the relaxing wisdom of the Gospel (Good News).
- To rejoice evermore is God's will for my life.

Sing a new song to the Lord! Sing it everywhere around the world. Sing out His praises! Bless His Name. Each day tell someone He saves.

Publish His glorious acts throughout the earth. Tell everyone about the amazing things He does. For the Lord is great beyond description and greatly to be praised.

Worship the Lord with the beauty of holy lives!

PSALM 96 TLB

Help us dear Lord, to publish the Good News that everyone will read by being living love letters from You to a sick and dying world.

Rejoice Evermore—God's will for a person's life in Jesus.

Do you agree that Jesus is a love letter from God to us?
❏ Yes   ❏ No

Do you agree that the Living Word, the Bible, is inerrant and completely true?   ❏ Yes   ❏ No

Are you true to His Word?   0-10 _____

Am I a living love letter in obedience to His Word? (Rom. 14:21,23)   ❏ Yes   ❏ No

If yes, use the other side of this page to write about yourself as a love letter to God. Then add a paragraph about how He will use you as a living epistle from Him to a sick and dying world.

If you are not a love letter, why not? Use the other side of this page to write why not. Then, pray that God will enable you to share your notes with someone who will pray with you. Invite the Holy Spirit to reveal to you specifically why you are unable at this time to be an epistle of God's grace and mercy.

Don't be discouraged! Look forward with anticipation and excitement to how Jesus' life recorded in the Bible and interpreted to you by the Holy Spirit will teach you to be His living epistle.

A good way to discover why you are unable to be a love letter from God to a sick and dying world may be the fact that you are not tithing your time to God. Use the Time Schedule which is on page 108 in this chapter. Ask God to help you account for your time each week. If you commit to tithing your time to the Lord each week you may begin to see yourself as a love letter from Him to a sick and dying world. As your spiritual life comes in order, biblical intimacy with God develops and your time becomes infinitely more productive for Him. Living productively for Him is dying to live abundantly in the love, joy and peace of the Lord at 40 - 50 - 60 - 70 - 80 - 90 and 100+!

CHAPTER 9

Peace is Freedom in Christ

Stand fast therefore, in the liberty by which Christ has made us free, and do not be entangled again with the yoke of bondage.

GALATIANS 5:1 NKJV

A s a living love letter from God and His reputation here on earth, I experience a new freedom. Each day I live is an opportunity for a new adventure because I am redeemed from sin by Jesus' death and resurrection. His sacrificial death granted me pardon...freedom! I delight in daily opportunities to practice this freedom in Christ. In Jesus, I am unencumbered by fear, anger, boredom, and other emotional bondage which would imprison me and other 40+ Christians.

Peace is freedom in Christ. I have been taught by the Holy Spirit from the Word of God that when I have peace that passes all understanding I am in the directive will of God. I have freedom. Allow me to share with you...

I adventure into each day—something I did not do before Jesus became my way, truth, and life. I now begin each day with the peace of God.

Peace I leave with you, My peace I give you; not as the world gives do I give to you. Let not your heart be troubled, neither let it be afraid.

JOHN 14:27 NKJV

Peace is the center of my position in and practice of freedom in Christ. Peace is also a sign to me of being in God's directive will. Before Jesus, I invariably ran ahead of God, then looked back over my shoulder and asked God to bless what I had already done, including sins I committed. Before I came to know Jesus in situations where I exerted my will, I never had peace with God. There was always an uneasiness, as though I had deliberately disobeyed God's Word (which of course I had). I have discovered that zest for life or a new adventure in living that is in any way disobedient to God will always fail.

I have been taught by the Holy Spirit from the Word of God that when I have peace that passes all understanding I am in the directive will of God. I have freedom.

Conversely, new exciting adventures in Jesus are the benchmark of each day lived in loving obedience to His Word (John 14:21).

First, by God's agape love and grace comes a sense of security and peace in knowing who I am and why I am here. Secondly, I appropriate the blessing of being in Him in order to do His will for my life. Self discovery in Jesus is exciting.

I have discovered I have become an epistle of the Good News of the Gospel. I can best describe what is happening to me as imperceptible amplitude[1], like Moses coming down from the Mount after being in the presence of God. There is a quietness of spirit, and peace within me that apparently is clearly evident to others, without awareness on my part. Moses didn't know that his face shone because he had been in the presence of God. People are able to perceive peace in others especially when they themselves do not have peace. Peace is our position in and practice of liberty—our way to live out a sanctified life in Christ. Peace with God is love in action. Biblically, peace is a verb, an action word. In Webster's New Universal Unabridged Dictionary peace is also defined as a noun:

- freedom from war or civil strife.
- a treaty or agreement to end, (be free from) war
- freedom from public disturbance or disorder, public security; law and order

---

[1] Christ-Centered Personality Development, Dr. Robert Abarno, Copyright 1988, Second Edition 1992, Third Edition 1994, Fourth Edition 1996. All right reserved.

• freedom from disagreement or quarrels; harmony, concord, etc.

It is notable that peace is related to freedom in these definitions. Can I, do I, as a 76 year old Christian adventure forth each day with peace in my soul because of my liberty in Christ? Is God's peace my freedom? I conclude by the wisdom of God and my life experience that peace is freedom! Jesus has set me free! Yet I ask myself, is freedom in Jesus absolute or relative?

In my soul I measure freedom (liberty), by the absence of anger and strife within me. In Jesus at 76 I have peace with God, self, and others. Therefore in Jesus freedom is absolute not relative. Biblical absolutes confirm my security that my freedom in Christ is not relative to anything in human nature or in the world.

Let the peace of God rule in your hearts...and be thankful.
COLOSSIANS 3:15

Paul said that we should be thankful! He mentions no conditions placed on this peace. The peace of God, the absolute truth that He simply is, rules my heart. What a relief it is not to struggle, not to be at war, within myself or with others. It is a blessing to have freedom from confusion, disorder, disagreements, dissension. Peace is being in the center of God's will for my life.

Struggling against God's will requires energy to initiate and maintain anger and strife. Age is a powerful blessing through which I have learned from painful experience that energy is wasted by being expended in anger and strife. Time and energy are too precious to be wasted!

Unlike struggling, peace is not energy- and time-demanding. Peace is energy-replenishing, so that time (the intimate moment eternal)[2] can be used joyfully, productively. The peace of God is synonymous with holiness and is a significant indicator of holiness.

---

[2] Ibid.

Those who are skeptics immediately attempt to reject anyone who conceptualizes themselves as holy. But my holiness, my sanctification rests not in myself but in what Jesus did and said so boldly and deliberately:

And for their sakes I sanctify Myself, that they may be sanctified (holy) by the truth.

JOHN 17:19

I Am the Way, the Truth and the Life.

JOHN 14:6

Many Christians, including myself, have great difficulty in personalizing what Jesus said in His Word. How can it be that He would want to make us holy as He is Holy? We seem to be captive to this humanistic world and unable to accept God's gift of peace from the Prince of Peace. We can fulfill the position and practice the liberty we have in Christ by being filled with His peace here on earth by faith. God's peace is precious to Christians who have experienced the presence of the Holy Spirit in their lives. Foregoing this peace in favor of anxiety and fear can weaken a Christian's faith. Instead of resting in their trust of Jesus and the peace of God, fear and anxiety take control of their lives.

The peace of God is synonymous with holiness and is a significant indicator of holiness.

Peace is a fruit of the Holy Spirit identified in Paul's letter to the Galatians (5:22-23). Peace is essential in the process of sanctification. Fearing rejection in this decade of persecution, many Christians are reluctant to make the process of sanctification the operating force of their lives. As with Moses coming down from the Mount after being in the presence of God, so with us, the power of Jesus' peace and holiness can shine forth to others through this "imperceptible amplitude."[3]

---

3   Ibid, 1.

In the holiness of the Lord this amplitude can become evident as we live each day in peace through the freedom Christ gives us. If we understand that sanctification is imparted to us by His grace, then we have the peace of God as a growing, maturing dynamic in our lives. The peace of God became apparent in my life after I turned 40, but is even more evident as I continue to age. There is within my being His holy peace that is awesome and best described as my freedom in Christ.

Peace came first with my salvation then became a significant part of my Christian life. I like to think of it like geography. There is a God-granted independent "state" of peace within my being that has become part of the other "states" of love and joy to form the "united states of sanctification" within me. As I age other parts of my being (mind, will, emotions) are maturing to full statehood as well. Patience, gentleness, goodness, faithfulness, meekness, and self control (Gal.5:22-23) become my biblical "union" in eternal spiritual "communion" with God.

To surrender completely and to be a holy, loving Christ-like person was a difficult reformation for me (Gen.1:26-27). To be worldly, negative, defensive, and disobedient was my natural man state before salvation. Early in my Christian life I was like some of my patients who are more inclined to be in rebellion and disobedient than to have love, joy and peace. The question for everyone is whether the world is lord or Jesus is Lord? Also, do we Christians "churchify" His sanctification rather than identify with, accept and live in communion with His Word?

And for their sakes I sanctify Myself, that they also may be sanctified by the truth.

JOHN 17:19

Our godly purpose is to be at peace which is our freedom in Christ. Our pride has another master. Who has control? Is the Holy Spirit in charge of our lives?

Jesus is our acknowledged King and Lord. However, Satan desires to implant in our mind, heart, and spirit prideful fear, anger and doubt about the efficacy of being sanctified, being holy and righteous by Jesus' sacrificial death (John 17:19, 10).

My soliloquy becomes something like this. How would my family and church react if I were to say at a testimony time "I am holy like Jesus?" (John 17:10). They know me, so rejection of my statement would be the response from family and church.

Surrendering to this rejection I become a rejector of the peace of God. My position and practice of freedom in Christ falls by the wayside. I am of my own volition bound, manacled, and imprisoned in prideful fear and anger. I have shut out the peace of Jesus from my life. As I age I become bored with my life. I ask myself what has happened to the adventure of self-discovery, the dynamic agape love of Jesus in my life? I despair.

Then God's Holy Spirit lovingly reminds me to confess, repent, and turn back to the Lord Jesus. Although at times I despair and am bored yet I know I can never be defeated in Christ. Jesus said:

> I will never leave you nor forsake you, so we can boldly say, The Lord is my helper, I will not fear. What can man do to me?
>
> HEBREWS 13: 5-6

As we age we seem to become less resistant and more vulnerable to Satan. Although we have more time to converse and witness to others, we often end up commiserating with them about our illnesses or theirs. Sadly we engage in a "pity party" and try to rationalize our own rejection (Gen.3:12). We fail to engage others in intimate exciting conversation about the Lord Jesus and forget that individually we are Jesus' glory here on earth (John 17:10). My role in Jesus is to be a living love letter from Him to a sick and dying world—alive, bright, full of warmth, and enthusiasm! Am I that kind of love letter? Am I being accountable as His glory, His reputation?

In consultation with my patients, I have repeatedly experienced a sense of rejection of God's peace by these hurting people. Peace is often absent in the lives of those who come to my office for counseling. "Peace, peace, there is no peace," is their heart's cry. Despite feelings and painful negative emotions, peace, the gift of Jesus, is our position and practice of freedom in Christ.

In counseling these Christians I listen to histories, significant events, feelings, emotions, and trivia which appear to be important to the patient. However, if I suggest that the Prince of Peace, by virtue of who He is and that what He has said, can restore peace in our lives the patient immediately becomes defensive. They invariably say they are inadequate because they have lost trust in Jesus. Christians revert to adopting the world's view of Jesus and themselves. The world again becomes more important than trusting God despite the truth that trust is inherent in our decision to accept Jesus as Savior and Lord (Ps.31:1). We often yield to the humanistic world.

Ungodly thinking and living, deeply ingrained in us by exposure to a humanistic world, is virtually impossible to displace in our own strength because it is constantly being reinforced everyday of our lives. We become preoccupied with the clamor and glamour of the world. We allow intrusion of the world through TV and print media to quench the Holy Spirit which is resident within us.

However, if each day we stand before God in His image and likeness and yield in obedience to His Word and His Holy Spirit as our loving teachers, our humanistic carnal habits and the contamination of the world will cease to exist! The Holy Spirit will not be quenched, but will continue to speak to us softly, quietly, always exhorting us to appropriate our riches in glory through Jesus our Lord. Peace will return.

Now the Lord is that Spirit; and where the Spirit of the Lord is, there is liberty.

2 CORINTHIANS 3:17

As I age I find it so much easier to stop and listen to the

Holy Spirit. I meditate each day to appropriate the specific teaching and exhortation of the Spirit for me. I have discovered there is more time to worship, praise, and thank the Lord than ever before. What is even more amazing is that I accomplish more each day when I follow the leading of the Holy Spirit than if I do not take time for direction by the Holy Spirit. What I do accomplish each day surprises me with love, joy, and peace! I do not attribute this to age alone but to who I am becoming in Jesus.

I work 50+ hours a week. I continue to write, publish, teach, consult, and advise as a living love letter from God to a sick and dying world. God is, therefore in Jesus, I am. What wonderful security God has provided for those who love Him and His Son Jesus, our Savior and Lord.

God is, therefore in Jesus, I am. My old carnal nature would have me be proud of this fact. But I am beginning to bear the fruit of humility so that my whole purpose in life is to give all glory and honor to the Lord Jesus. I can hardly accept what is happening to me. No longer am I bound and tempted by this world. I am actively engaged by the beauty of the life God has given me. The pleasures of the world which constantly bombard me as the "ideal" for every man, woman, and child I am able to discern as lies of Satan. I simply do not believe that this humanistic egocentric world with all of its well-advertised attractions, can distract me from my basic life purpose which is to be like Jesus and do God's will for my life in Him.

With great joy I have discovered I am a publication from God which gives me a profound sense of purpose. I am beginning to understand why God has permitted me to live for 76 years. I wonder, as Abraham and Moses wondered, how God could use me at 80, 90, and 100+? I think the answer is contained in Psalm 78 (TLB):

O My people listen to my teaching. Open your ears to what I am saying. For I will show you lessons from our history, stories handed down to us from former generations. I will reveal these truths to you so that you can describe these glorious deeds of Jehovah to your children, and tell them about the mighty miracles He did. For He gave His laws to Israel, and commanded our fathers to teach them to their children, so that they in turn could teach their children too. Thus His laws pass down from generation to generation. In this way, each generation has been able to obey His laws and to set its hope anew on God and not forget His glorious miracles.

P S A L M   7 8 : 1 - 7

At 76 I am being released by God from my professional counseling practice and becoming equipped by His grace to teach and share application of and accountability for His Word. I am enabled to communicate and publish His glorious miracles (Ps.96 TLB) which He has written in and through our lives.

By His grace, love and mercy Christians are enabled in His peace to enjoy our position and practice of eternal liberty in Christ. Praise God!

Peace in Jesus is our eternal security and a way to carry out the Great Commission (Matt.

> *My basic life purpose is to be like Jesus and do God's will for my life in Him.*

28:19,20; Acts 1:8) with vigor, enthusiasm, and great joy! What a wonderful discovery paradigm for my life in Jesus! My age does not detract from but specifically enhances peace as my freedom in Christ—freedom from anxiety, fear, pride, and boredom, freedom to trust totally in Him for today and the days ahead. Praise God from whom all blessings flow!

Do not let age be a deterrent. Commit your eternal life (John 17:3) this day to know the Prince of Peace and enjoy your unique position and ability to practice liberty and freedom in Christ.

How much liberty do I have in Jesus Christ to practice my faith?   0 - 10 _____

Is my liberty in Jesus setting me free from the fear of aging?   ❏ Yes   ❏ No

Based on Gal. 5:1-12, 13-15, how am I practicing my liberty in Jesus?

- •
- •
- •
- •

Am I the living in liberty and manifesting the fruit of the Holy Spirit ? (Gal. 5:22-23)
Love   0 - 10 _____
Joy   0 - 10 _____
Peace   0 - 10 _____

If the fruits of the Holy Spirit are not evident in your life please indicate below in writing why not?

Plan the next 7, 14, 21 years of your life in Christ. Use 7 year segments. Anticipate with God's peace the position and practice of liberty you have in Christ. Love, joy, and peace are the fruit seed of personal reformation. Age is no excuse before God not to become a personal reformation in Jesus. Now is the accepted time! Pray, devote, praise, worship, then record your plan. Keep in mind the lives of Abraham, Moses, Caleb, Anna, and others.

Plan 7 years . . . (Use a separate piece of paper or more for each 7-year plan).
Plan the next 7 years . . .
Plan the next 7 years . . .

In the next chapter we look at the comfort of eternal life with Jesus who is our resurrection life. The love, joy, and peace in the Lord at 40, 50, 60, 70, 80, 90, 100+ is our blessed assurance, or if you prefer, insurance underwritten by God for our eternal security in Him (John 3:16).

Christians have a non-revocable insurance policy that eternal life is the reality of our resurrection (John 17:3). With this knowledge, we can proceed to communicate our position and practice of liberty in Christ. We become living love letters from God to those who do not know Jesus as Savior and Lord. We are dying as we age which is our present crucifixion only to live abundantly, our resurrection, in the love, joy, and peace of the Lord.

God is pleased that what He has done by creating us in His image and likeness is very good (Gen.1:31). As we age as breathing, living, walking epistles from God we reflect the image and likeness of Jesus (Gen. 1:26,27) to a sick and dying world. As we age delightfully from 40-100+ in the love, joy, and peace of the Lord we live out our obedience to God (John 14:21,23). Then, His overwhelmingly glory is reflected in and through us as His reputation here on earth. Praise God!

CHAPTER 10

Eternal Life With Jesus
The Love, Joy and Peace of the Lord at 40, 50, 60, 70, 80, 90, 100+ Has Only Just Begun

Francis Schaeffer asked the question, "How Should We Then Live?"[1]. I like the directness of that question. Biblically, the question leaves no room for dissimulation or rationalization.

At 76 I have contemplated dying (crucifixion) and simultaneously meditated on dying to live eternally (resurrection). In Chapter 4, "Without Jesus it is boring to grow old", I referred to E. Kubler-Ross, M.D. (1969), who delineated a construct of the five stages of dying and death:

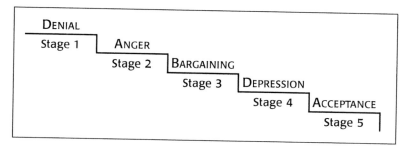

DENIAL
Stage 1   ANGER
      Stage 2   BARGAINING
            Stage 3   DEPRESSION
                  Stage 4   ACCEPTANCE
                        Stage 5

For the humanist man/woman the stages of dying are the only rites of passage from life to eternal death simply because humanist man/woman's life is limited to their time here on earth. But for Christians eternal life in Jesus begins here and now on earth and continues for eternity in His agape love (John 3:16). For the 40+ Christian this means that eternal life is now —

---

[1] Francis A. Schaeffer, How Should We Then Live? Fleming Revell Company, Old Tappan, N.J., 1976.

$\mathcal{B}$ut for Christians eternal life in Jesus begins here and now on earth and continues for eternity.

at 40+— not something that begins at your physical death.

During his or her lifetime God's process of sanctification for the Christian's life is positively different from the bare negative existence of the humanist. Unlike the humanist, Christians are privileged to follow Jesus and enjoy eternal life. Christians are empowered by God's Word and Holy Spirit to die to self and to live with joy now and for eternity (John 3:16).

For the humanist this world is all there is and life ends at death. Joyfully for the Christian physical death is only transitional, from crucifixion to resurrection!

Through the Lord's mercies we are not consumed,
Because His compassion's fail not.
They are new every morning.
Great is Your faithfulness.

LAMENTATIONS 3:22,23

Time for me is always t̲he i̲ntimate m̲oment e̲ternal.[2]—very precious and to be enjoyed, not wasted! My mother, the Grand Dame of Chapter 1, never mentioned time or age during the last five years of her life. Mother did not believe in wasting time by feeling old or useless even at 98. She was productively engaged with the Lord right up until that momentary pause before she entered fully into His presence.

Mother understood that time is precious and should never be wasted in sorrow and self-pity. There are many thousands of 40+ persons who are disabled by depression and therefore vulnerable to wasting precious time. These folks are accountable to God and to themselves for creative use of the time God has given them. A wonderful resolution for depression is to spend

---

[2] Christ-Centered Personality Development, Dr. Robert Abarno, ©1988, Second Edition 1992, Third Edition 1994, Fourth Edition 1996. All rights reserved.

time communicating with God in praise, worship, adoration, and petition for others.

As Christians, we need to tithe our time as well as our money. There are thousands of people 40+, even those with physical disabilities like Mother, who are motivated by the Holy Spirit to use their time productively in service to God. Eternal life does not begin when we die, but at that moment in Jesus, we are reborn for eternity.

We rarely hear eternal life discussed outside preaching services or teaching seminars. In order to understand eternal life we must believe

Joyfully for the Christian physical death is only transitional, from crucifixion to resurrection!

the Bible is inerrant and therefore not fear death as the end of our existence. Eternal life by God's infinite wisdom supersedes dying. I pray and ask the Holy Spirit to continue to remind me and my patients that Satan never ceases to distort our biblical orientation, development, and maturity so that we can't think of eternal life without first thinking of our own death. What does God say in His Word?

> *Therefore, if anyone is in Christ, he is a new creation; old things have passed away; behold, all things have become new.*
>
> 2 CORINTHIANS 5:17

A Christian's spiritual birth in Jesus precedes physical death and continues unabated for eternity (John 3:16). Our soul/personality (mind, will, and emotions), our God-created uniqueness never dies and is never lost. We cannot be separated from Him, here and now or for eternity. Someone might ask, how can you be so certain? Aging in the love and joy of the Lord is peaceful (being at peace is being in the center of God's directive will) and is rooted and grounded in the fact that the Bible is inerrant, absolute truth. Biblical inerrancy gives me freedom from humanistic constructs like that postulated by Kubler-Ross. which suggest, notwithstanding the reality of death, a fatal hopeless decline without eternal life in view

People who do not know Jesus exist in this world as a natural man, woman or child with an expected life span of 70+ years. But the love, joy, and peace of the Lord has no end. Life in Jesus is eternal. When we accept Jesus as Savior and Lord we are sometimes tempted by Satan as we are transitioned from the natural to the spiritual individual. Emphasis on the physical body with all its demands for ease and pleasure seem to require constant attention. We become preoccupied with age, the physical and emotional demands of our body and the unremitting demands of society. Therefore we fail to fully appropriate the eternal significance of our spiritual birth. We are inclined to subordinate our new creation in Jesus (2 Cor. 5:17) to the old routine of our sinful soul, body, and spirit.

Life in Jesus is eternal.

Paul, who as Saul experienced sin, cried out in anguish and desperation as we so often do as he wrote Romans 7 and examined his wretched state of self-condemnation " for I know that in me...that is in my flesh nothing good dwells," (Rom. 7:18). Paul understood how eros had occupied his soul (mind, will, and emotions)—literally his life.

At 40+ we seem to say like Paul did, "O wretched man that I am". We express our despair and our dismay about the aging process and thereby block Jesus out of our lives. There is a sense of hopelessness in us about aging and dying. At 40+ we are convinced by the secular world that we are "over the hill"— essentially useless to ourselves and to others.

O wretched man that I am! Who will deliver me from the body of death? I thank God— through Jesus Christ our Lord! So then, with the mind I myself serve the law of God, but with the flesh the law of sin.

ROMANS 7:24,25

Then Paul rejoiced in his (and our) position and practice of freedom in Christ. Paul thanked God through Jesus Christ as he fully appropriated His eternal life by completely yielding to the Holy Spirit:

> So now we can obey God's laws if we follow after the Holy Spirit and no longer obey the old evil nature within us.

Those who let themselves be controlled by their lower natures (the customs and beliefs of this secular humanistic world), live only to please themselves, but those who follow after the Holy Spirit find themselves doing things that please God. Following after the Holy Spirit leads to life (eternal) and peace, but following after the old nature leads to (permanent) death.

> Yet, even though Christ lives within you, your body will die because of sin, but your spirit will live, for Christ has pardoned it. And if the Spirit of God, who raised up Jesus from the dead, lives in you, He will make your dying bodies live again (in resurrected bodies) after you die, by means of this same Holy Spirit (which you received at your salvation in Jesus) living within you.

> ROMANS 8:4-6, 10-11 TLB

This book was written using the age of 40 as the point of departure from being young to beginning to age. Our contemporary humanistic society has established 40 as the beginning of our physical and emotional demise. However, if we live, move, and have our being in Jesus nothing can be further from God's truth! (John 3:16)

By the evil power of Satan and our daily exposure to a humanistic world view we are tempted to resign ourselves to human aging, the dying and death process, not to eternal life. Therefore we are led to disbelieve God's Word which states Jesus is eternal (John 3:16) and that in Him we are eternal. He is the Way, the Truth, and the Life (John 14:6). Paul, by God's Holy Spirit, reveals to us that in Jesus:

We do not walk according to the flesh (eternal death) but according to the Spirit.

ROMANS 8:4B NKJV

Christians age joyfully in Jesus as they meditate on living and walking eternally in the Holy Spirit and not just in the flesh. In Jesus, we have literally passed from death —the fear, emphasis and transientness of physical death—to eternal life which God has provided for us in His agape love.

For if you live according to the flesh you will die; but if by the Spirit you put to death the deeds of the body, you will live.

ROMANS 8:13 NKJV

If I cast aside my impending physical death as the most significant event of my life, and instead, continue to live in the agape love of God, then I live with joy and peace eternally. As I experience aging which is the crucifixion of my physical body I remain secure in the biblical truth that Jesus has overcome death for me. He has given me eternal life which begins when a person commits their life to Him.

My position on crucifixion (the aging and impending death of my physical body) and the concurrent transition to the continuing process of eternal life is based upon the truth of the Bible. I am biblically convinced that the love, joy, and peace of the Lord at 40+ (or any age in Jesus) is dying to self to live abundantly. My life in Jesus is biblical reality not humanistic worldly rationalization, i.e., hedonism.

For the first 32 years of my life I was convinced that death is something fearful and abhorrent. In my natural man that seemed to be understandable, even reasonable. However, a natural man's understanding and knowledge are limited and immature in light of the infinite wisdom of the Holy Spirit and the Bible. At age 32 I accepted Jesus as my Savior and Lord. Jesus then became the unfolding love, joy and peace of my eternal life.

I do not attempt here to introduce a new concept that is designed to be popular. I have heard those who express with horror and fear that death is the end of everything. To those outside of Jesus who I have observed, eternal life is unimportant and insignificant, until such time as they face death. At that point in time everyone who is close to death cries out, "God help me!" God is suddenly front and center in their lives.

So the reality choice I have made about my impending death is not to suggest to the reader some kind of spiritual placebo. My choice is for Jesus and the love, joy, and peace I have in Him here and now and for eternity. My choice is the truth of the Word of God. My choice rests on the fact that life has only just begun for me and anyone else whose commitment is to Jesus Christ. Eternity cannot be measured by time or it would not be eternity. God is not temporal, He is infinite. So in Him, in His image and likeness here and now and for eternity, I live and have my being with great joy (Gen. 1:26,27).[3] In Jesus physical death is just a transition, a pause, like a millisecond between breaths.

The reader might think that one must continue to take action to retain eternal life. No! In my decision at 32 to take Jesus as Savior and Lord of my life I made the decision I needed to make. His promise of eternal life for me began at 32 and has continued unabated. Forty four years later I am more alive than ever in Him!

This book gives written expression to what I cannot con-

---

[3] "And this is eternal life, that they may know (ginosko) Thee, the only true God, and Jesus Christ whom Thou hast sent." (John 17:3 NAS)

  − accepting Christ as your personal Savior is only the beginning of the journey and not the end

  − NB: ginosko is different from oida even though they are translated as "know" in the English language (Vines's Expository Dictionary of Biblical Words p. 436). Ginosko means the inception or progress in "knowledge" and oida means the fullness of "knowledge."

    i.e., (John 8:55 NAS) "and you have come to know (ginosko) Him, but I know (oida) Him; and if I say that I do not know (oida) Him, I shall be a liar like you, but I do know (oida) Him and keep His Word."

tain (Jer.20:9). By His grace, I experience each day Holy Spirit comfort, the comfort of eternal life with Jesus, not the fires of eternal death and hell. Jesus has given me assurance that I will pause only for a millisecond when my crucifixion is complete, and then take the next breath in resurrected eternal life with Jesus.

Death is swallowed up in victory. O death, where is your sting? O Hades where is your victory?
1 CORINTHIANS 15:54-55

These things I have spoken to you, that in Me you may have peace. In the world you will have tribulation; but be of good cheer, I have overcome the world.
JOHN 16:33

Those of us who are 40+ do not need to be apprehensive about aging. Aging is a time of excitement, a new eternal adventure in the Lord. In God's timing a new body will be prepared for us that will never age or die. God gave Peter, James, and John a preview of Jesus' transfigured resurrected body. Similarly, our transformed heavenly body will be beautiful and perfect (Matt. 17:1). All my human worldly questions have ceased in joyful anticipation of what the God of eternity has prepared for me. I look forward with great anticipation, (not with dread and apprehension), about being with Jesus for eternity in my transfigured heavenly body. Praise God!

> *Aging is a time of excitement, a new eternal adventure in the Lord.*

APPLICATION & ACCOUNTABILITY

Do you believe that your crucifixion ends in physical death?   ❑ Yes   ❑ No

Do you believe that God is preparing a resurrected body for you that will never age or die?   ❑ Yes   ❑ No

Is eternal life in Jesus your reality here and now? (John 3:16)   ❑ Yes   ❑ No

Is eternal life here and now full of the love, joy, and peace of the Lord?   ❑ Yes   ❑ No
If not, describe in writing why not? Be honest with yourself and God.

Pray to God in Jesus' name to help you appropriate the love, joy, and peace of the Lord. Jesus said, "I have come to give you life and give it to you abundantly." (John 10:10b) Allow Him to reveal Himself to you as you obey His Word (John 14:21,23) then watch as He manifests Himself to you. God is awesome and compassionate with love, mercy, and grace.

Know in your soul that real Biblical intimacy with God is eternal life.

Yield to the leading of His Holy Spirit. God is Sovereign in your life as a Christian (Ex.20:3).

Be comforted and discover in reality moment by moment that you have eternal life in Jesus in your life here and now. Biblical intimacy with God is manifested by dying to self to live abundantly in the love, joy, and peace of the Lord.

CHAPTER 11

~

The Summit of Our Faith is His Holiness

For the first 32 years of my life I barely existed under the stronghold of humanistic despair. Then, I was introduced to Jesus and my eternal life began. However, I labored under a new-found discipline in the church called legalism (Gr. nomos). Some churches exhibit form and structure under the guise of Christian love. This type of love is not agape but Phariseeical in its demands for strict compliance to the laws of men and strict adherence to tradition, not to the Spirit of the Word of God. In the beginning, legalism offered me a measure of security as I was absorbed in the business of "laboring for Jesus" and legalistic self-righteousness. But, much to my chagrin I discovered that my new life in Jesus was not the summit of a faith but a rapid descent into the deep canyon of nomos. My life resonated with bondage for myself, my family, and others. Legalism bound me tightly in my formative spiritual development.

I didn't recognize that I was spiritually in bondage and my development in Jesus had faded away. I was even unaware of my self-righteousness except for exhortations from others that I should love as Jesus loved me (John 15:12). God was faithful to hear these exhortations and prayers on my behalf. By His Word (John 17:19), I was released from my prison cell in the canyon of legalism and transformed by His Holy Spirit to be faithful, and thus experience the summit of faith—His holiness.

I was taught the difference between God's agape love, eros and nomos. Eros was easily recognized because that had been my condition in the world without Jesus. However, nomos was much more subtle and it is only by God's grace and mercy that I was able to break free of legalism in the church and in my personal life.

Jesus never abandoned me despite my self-righteousness. Jesus in His infinite wisdom knew that prior to my salvation I never had anything to be self-righteous about. Jesus has committed never to leave or forsake me! (Heb 13:5) He has filled me with His Holy Spirit, and as I "leak," He refills me. He is the breath of my life and the beat of my heart. In Him I move and have my being.

As a result of His faithfulness, my faith in Jesus, like a seed, has grown and become dynamic (Eph. 6:10), bearing fruit (Gal. 5:22-23). My eternal dynamic life in Jesus has even penetrated the concrete of self-righteousness and stubbornness. The sustenance and the development of my seed of faith is the Bible. Daily I am strengthened by the power of the Living Word by faith to climb the mountain toward the summit—His holiness!

In this chapter, I do not suggest a protocol or procedure for holiness but merely share experiences in my life at 40+ which are analogous to reaching heights of love, joy, and peace that eluded me in my earlier life. Following my birth in Jesus at 32 I was still too oriented to the busyness of the world to begin to absorb being in Jesus. I went through the motions and constraints of legalism following my conversion and was thereby diverted from the love, joy, and peace of the Lord. My business and my legalism fit together nicely. However, I knew something was missing.

By faith I was convinced of the inerrancy of scripture. God is Sovereign! Therefore, secularism cannot exist if God is Sovereign.

Seven years after my conversion I was infilled by the Holy Spirit. I remembered that when I had accepted Jesus as my Savior that I received the Holy Spirit. However, I knew nothing of the person and work of the Holy Spirit. In the church in which I was involved for the first seven years of my Christian life, the Holy Spirit was acknowledged but not taught. Finally, as I was introduced to the person and work of the Holy Spirit, legalism faded, and the climb to the summit of holiness began in earnest. As I was guided and directed by the Holy Spirit I began to understand the Bible in text and context. By faith I was convinced of the inerrancy of scripture. God is Sovereign! Therefore, secularism cannot exist if God is Sovereign.

Then the process of sanctification (Gal.5:22-23)— developing the fruit of the Holy Spirit enabled me to understand (John 17:19 TLB):

I consecrate Myself to meet their need for growth in truth and holiness.

Yet still, at times, legalism clutches me in its grip. Although unintentional I slip back down the mountain toward the canyon and the imprisonment out of which I had been lifted by God's grace and forbearance. He knows my heart, he made it. He knows my mind, will, and emotions, my yearning to communicate to others the love, joy, and peace of the Lord by which I live (Ps.96). So He continues to allow me in faith (James 2:14-18) to press on up the mountain to the summit as I experience His love and grace. At 76 the view I have as I approach the summit is breathtaking!

Chapter 6 is titled, "Aging: a time of Self Discovery. Get involved in living eternally with Jesus—life is a great adventure!" is true! I have found life in Jesus to be a great adventure. It is like the whole world unfolding in a multiplicity of dimensions, *ad infinitum*. I can best illustrate what I mean by relating how on a Sunday afternoon returning from a short holiday at the beach my wife looked up to the sky through her sunglasses and discovered an unfolding of the heavens beyond description.

Ann was awe struck, literally overwhelmed by the pure majesty of God's creation! Upon recovering from the unfolding vista of the heavens before her, Ann urged me to look and see what she had seen. Hers was a joyous plea for confirmation.

The lenses in her sunglasses were designed to block ultraviolet rays and enhance the first, second, and third or more dimensions for the viewer. When I put on her sunglasses they did exactly what they were designed to do. At first I blinked my eyes because I have never seen anything like what I saw. Driving the car at 55 miles per hour became autonomic while we attempted to visually absorb the multi-dimensional beauty God displayed before us. In one state I was performing the necessary function of driving the car, but at the same time I experienced in my heart and emotions what I understood to be a heavenly state of being. If we could envision the second coming of Christ as described in 1Thess. 4:16-18; Rev.21:1-3, what God allowed Ann and me to see was a preview of what is to come for those who love Him.

When I looked up into the heavens I described to Ann what I was seeing as she had previously described to me what she had seen. As the rays of the sun poured through the manifold layers of clouds the sun rays appeared to be highways from the heavens to the earth. There were distinct paths, wide rays of sunlit luminescent highways, descending and ascending, as they permeated the clouds.

The indescribable beauty of the heavens reached down to earth for what looked like a mile, but only from the left side of the highway. In front, and to the right of our car the sky was filled with cumulus clouds floating freely through the blue sky in majestic progression as though attending from the farthest reaches of the heavens the display of God's awesome might and power. These magnificent clouds provided a framework of incredible beauty for the miracle in slow motion of descending and ascending sunrays on center stage.

As we moved along the highway we experienced a time of absolute quiet which seemed perfectly appropriate as we observed the majesty of God. As the sun rays began to fade Ann expressed her understanding of this event as analogous to the transfiguration vignette. We imagined the scene when Jesus revealed Himself to Peter, James, and John on the Mount of Transfiguration.

Jesus took Peter, James, and John his brother, brought them up on a high mountain by themselves, and was transfigured before them. His face shone like the sun, and His clothes became as white as the light.

MATTHEW 17:1,2

We felt we had been in the presence of the Lord although we did not see Him or hear Him speak. He had granted us an audience into His Almighty presence. We weren't busy "doing" anything. We were just "being" in His Presence, and for us it was reward beyond description. We experienced dimension upon dimension of His unfolding majesty, might, and power. We felt such love, joy, and peace in the Lord that we were for those several minutes literally transformed into His Holy Presence.

Ann and I together, as one body, of which Jesus is the acknowledged Head, enjoyed a summit experience in Jesus' limitless love and holiness. Jesus was so kind, by manifesting Himself so beautifully to us expecting nothing from us in return (John 15:12). All we could say was "Lord Jesus, we stand in awe of You. We agape You!"

Later, I thought about the two states of doing and being. Most of my life has been arrested within the prison routine of doing this and doing

> *Later, I thought about the two states of doing and being.*

that to comply with the contemporary humanistic world. Seldom have I discovered myself in the state of being in Jesus outside of this world. I had been caught up in my legalistic attitude and my busy and seemingly all important life. I have since concluded that I should **be** in Jesus (He is, therefore I am) in order to **do** His will.

I thought about my earlier life prior to becoming a Christian. Following my military service during WW II, I was engaged in business from 1946 until 1965. Then my life and career changed dramatically. I realized on July 4, 1952 when I was miraculously saved by Jesus Christ (my Independence Day from the world) that God had a plan for my life (Eph.1:3-12). Nothing made sense except to follow Jesus wherever He led. So began my climb to the summit with many slips, slides, falls, bumps, deep bruises, and near disasters along the Way, to the Truth and to eternal Life, even Jesus Christ. (John 14:6). At 76, I am still climbing but with renewed energy as I agape Him more each day and die to self to live abundantly in Him. My resurrection is in ascendancy as my crucifixion is in decline. I am being surprised by joy.

My resurrection is in ascendancy as my crucifixion is in decline. I am being surprised by joy.

I learned through His Word and the leading of His Holy Spirit that to "rejoice evermore is God's will for my life in Jesus!" I had never thought about rejoicing evermore or about the possibility of that state of being as reality for my life. Wonder of wonders. I also learned from the Bible that a living liturgy of love, joy and peace is reserved for me being in Jesus (1 Thess. 5:16-18):

- *Rejoice evermore*
- *pray without ceasing (unlimited communication)*
- *in everything (nothing left out) give thanks,*
- *for this is the will of God (who am I to argue?)*
- *in Christ Jesus for you.*

As I climb the mountain toward the summit rejoicing evermore I am not motivated by a "works" faith, rather by the hand and footholds which are with age increasingly apparent to me. I do not slip as often, I do not slide as far, there are less and less falls, bumps, and bruises. My feet are Holy Spirit-guided to seek out the footholds in the solid rock. I am less inclined to step on slippery, unstable places, always lovingly reminded by the Holy Spirit of the pain I suffered in the past for sin.

I have begun to discover that "peace is my position and practice of liberty in Christ Jesus" (chapter 9). I know by the power of the indwelling Holy Spirit that I am protected in this joyous climb to the summit. As I "position" myself for the next step, and look forward to the step after that, I "practice" with each movement "the liberty I have in Christ Jesus."

At times I am tempted to look down. However, all of my life I have in one way or another looked down, taken a peek at things below and rationalized I could better assess my position by comparison with where I had come from. The temptation of looking at where I had been in sin did nothing to help me proceed with confession and repentance, onward and upward to being like Jesus. I have abandoned downward in favor of looking upward to Him, who is awaiting me at the summit with agape love and open arms.

I am forty four years in the Lord, seven without the understanding and infilling of the Holy Spirit and then in the ensuing 37 years enjoying the blessings of His Holy Spirit and His Word. My climb to the summit has been one of seeing Him more clearly, and I conclude, "The summit of my faith is His Holiness." He is teaching me to be holy as He is Holy.

This ascent toward the top of the mountain is a very personal experience that I share inadequately. The climb to the summit is highly intimate, based upon our God created-uniqueness, our individual personality/soul (mind, will, and emotions). "God is a Jealous God" (Ex.34:14). The love, joy, and peace individually expressed by "our faith" become the steps in Jesus, the solid rock leading to "the summit which is His Holiness."

In worship, praise, and adoration we can experience the Holiness and Glory of the Lord God Almighty as Moses did on Mount Sinai (Ex.24: 13ff). Truly, as with Moses, so with us, the summit of our faith is His holiness, witnessed, seen, experienced, lived and enjoyed!

> Then the Lord spoke to Moses, saying, And let them make Me a sanctuary, that I may dwell among them.
>
> *EXODUS 25:1, 8*

God appeared to Solomon by night as He confirmed the Davidic Covenant (1 Kings 3:2-9).

> *I have heard your prayer, and have chosen this place for Myself as a house of sacrifice...If my people who are called by My name will humble themselves, and pray and seek my face, and turn from their wicked ways, then I will forgive their sin and heal their land. Now My eyes will be open and My ears attentive to prayer made in this place. For now I have chosen and sanctified (John 17:19) this house, that My name may be there forever, and My eyes and My heart will be there perpetually.*
>
> 2 CHRONICLES 7:14-16 NKJV

As our faith works toward the summit of His holiness (John 17:19) each of us becomes a tabernacle in which the Holy Spirit dwells. God told us that "His eyes will be open and His ears attentive to prayers made in this place." What place? The place in which His Holy Spirit lives—in us! As we become obedient to His Word, as we climb to the summit of faith, He reveals (manifests) Himself to us (John 14:21). We become His Glory, His reputation here on earth, as we will be some day in heaven.

As we become obedient to His Word, He reveals (manifests) Himself to us. We become His Glory, His reputation here on earth.

Moses descended from Mount Sinai at 80+ with an aura of holiness so apparent that he was asked by those who saw Him to veil his face. Moses had been in the presence of Jehovah, and his summit experience was clearly evident to all who knew him.

Moses' age was not an issue. His age was an asset which God used to glorify Himself. Here was a man who lived 40 years in Pharoah's palace, 40 years as a shepherd in the back of the desert, then 40 years leading the people of Israel in the wilderness. In all that time God did not leave or forsake Moses. God used Moses to glorify Himself. What a vital life Moses has as a friend of God! He never saw himself as "too old" by faith to mature in his own spiritual development.

For Moses when he was finally called at 120 to eternal life in Jesus, the love, joy, and peace of the Lord had only just begun! Later Moses in his resurrected body appeared with Jesus on the Mount of Transfiguration (Matt.17:1-3), at "peace" with Jesus, confirming "his position and practice of liberty in Christ."

Moses had two mountaintop experiences with God. Following the first experience Moses returned to the camp with His face aglow to carry out God's exhortation and commands as he led the Israelites. Moses had been with the Lord God Jehovah forty days and forty nights. Being in Jesus can be our experience as we reflect His image in our daily walk in this world. The summit of our faith is His Holiness.

We can "rejoice evermore" as we experience our eternal life in Jesus at 40-100+. Our transfiguration into our heavenly bodies with Jesus will follow! Our personality/soul (mind, will, and emotions), our God-created uniqueness will inhabit our heavenly bodies in Jesus' presence for eternity! Praise God!

REJOICE,
AGAIN I SAY
REJOICE!

At the end of each of the preceding chapters I inserted an Application and Accountability section. I thought it might be a good idea for me to share with you how the application of and accountability for faith is working out in my life.

As I wrote about the bumps and bruises of climbing the mountain of life toward the summit I was reminded by the Holy Spirit of the humor involved in aging. Some of the bumps and bruises along the way are really amusing.

I forget things from time to time. Now that would be stressful if I were younger. However, as I age I know I do not deliberately forget, it just seems to happen. I have discovered however that most of the times I forget, things seem to work better than if I had remembered the appointment, date, event, meeting, etc. It isn't that I desire to avoid responsibility but it is a little like when God does not immediately answer my anxious prayer. Somehow by His grace I manage to survive what I thought might be a disaster. I am not recommending forgetfulness, but in retrospect I do applaud God's watchcare, forbearance and protection for one who seeks to be responsible but who with age does not primarily meet the expectations of others. Some of the times of forgetfulness end up in laughter after I apologize and explain. There are no feelings within me of chagrin or frustration. I end up using the time productively for the Lord and myself.

I may be reachng and if I am I ask God and everyone else to forgive me. As time passes there seem to be more lapses but by God's grace and mercy I am more peaceable. In fact, by His grace some of the situations I would have been involved in by my own wisdom may have compromised my testimony. God has a sense of humor because in these missed appointments, dates, events or meetings I have become wiser either by His blessing or by His design. I have learned from Him to see things according to His priority and in His perspective. God continues to simplify my life.

Then there are other things which are humorous like not being embarassed in living or social situations in which I have" messed up". I am constantly amazed at the graciousness of God. He keeps me from stumbling when I fail to observe certain social ammenities and courtesies that in the past would have initiated stress for me and others. My perception of stress has diminished and has been replaced by a certain innocence. Guilelessness seems to develop with aging in the Lord.

I laugh at myself more. I am not so critical of myself and others. I enjoy the slowing down of schedule and time. The intimate moment eternal with God is truly that. God has helped me develop intimacy with Him. I am more biblically intimate with God. I spend much more time with Him now. I rejoice in prayer, thinking and writing. As a result I am a better friend to myself, to my wife and to others.

As I speak less often I have more time to observe. Taking time to observe people, animals, birds, trees, flowers, and events in everyday life with joy not as a judge or jury but with enthusiasm can only be generated in me by God.

Although I get angry at those who ignore or disobey God and His Word thereby hastening the decline of America, I do not remain angry. I know that God always wins in the end and that I am on the winning side which has not always been the case when I attempt to do things on my own. So I am pleasantly involved with contemporary life but essentially without stress.

I learn so much more because I am aging. I like to take time to learn which was not always the case in the past. In high school, college and university there was always pressure to feedback what I had been taught but rarely did I learn from this process. Now I enjoy studying the Bible, concordance, encyclopedias, history texts, biographies, my favorite authors and access to libraries though my computer.

There is a whole world of information out there which is accessible to me from my office or home. I enjoy learning on my own from all of these wonderful sources. I thank God for making all this information available to me (John 17:3; 2Pet.3:18b). I sometimes laugh at myself when I think of all the supposedly erudite things I said or wrote when I was much younger. I have discovered with much joy that aging in Jesus bears the fruit of reality and wisdom.

Application of my faith is very practical and rewarding. What God allows me to do I do In peace which is the accountability part of my faith. As I learn, grow and mature in the Lord I have freedom which I treasure. Then humor becomes an integral part of my freedom.

As I learn I sometimes get the notion I know something. Then in order to put my acquired knowledge into perspective I read the Bible and I laugh. Measured by the Word of God my knowledge is infinitesimal and I know it. I meditate with joy about who I am and why I am here according to His plan. (Gen.1:26,27,31).

It is wonderful to be able to enjoy my life and know that God is in charge. My peace and security rests in His infinite wisdom and power. I am Holy Spirit comforted by His agape love as I age with the love, joy and peace of the Lord. I am excited about what is ahead for me in Him! I have peace as I believe "I can do all things through Christ who strengthens me". (Phil.4:13)

CHAPTER 12

I Can Do All Things at Any Age Through Christ Who Strengthens Me

Hebrews 11 the faith chapter has always intrigued me. Men and women of faith are specifically identified by the Holy Spirit in Hebrews 11. These men and women are biblical models for me. Their lives are dynamic, committed, sanctified, and holy (John 17:19,10).

To understand the infinite wisdom of God in using these people of faith for His own glory is exciting. What is even more exciting is to know that I, too, can do all things through Christ who strengthens me! (Phil.4:13) So can you!

The potential and ability to do all things in Christ has become reality in my aging process. This is practical application of my faith. Earlier on in my life I was busy—too preoccupied with my worldly daily schedule to take the time or make the effort to study the lives of the biblical saints of God. I did not understand how God designed, created, and used them for His purposes and glory. I discovered they were never to busy for God to bless them as He used them.

Now I prayerfully follow the example of the writer of Hebrews 11 and suggest for those of us 40-100+ to consider these men and women of faith:

> Billy and Ruth Graham
> Mother Teresa
> Oswald Chambers
> Jeanne Guyon
> Matthew Henry
> H. A. Ironside

Wetherall A. Johnson
C. S. Lewis
Martyn Lloyd-Jones
Peter and Catherine Marshall
G. Campbell Morgan
A. W. Tozer
Andrew Murray
Watchman Nee
J. B. Phillips
J. I. Packer
Arthur Pink
John Knox
Hannah Whitall Smith
Charles Haddon Spurgeon
Francis and Edith Schaeffer
Lehman Strauss
R.A. Torrey
Bob and Judith Mumford
Henri J. M. Nouwen
Glenn Martin

Well, how much more do I need to say? (Heb.11:32TLB). A more knowledgeable Christian bible student than me could recount the even more faithful people God has designed, created, and used in His service. Is it possible for God to use you and me as He used these men and women of faith at 40, 50, 60, 70, 80, 90 and 100+?

Recently a man who is 68 asked me what I planned on doing with the last 10 % of my life. He informed me that statistically men live 70 years. Since I am 76 I have lived beyond the three score and ten years allotted to man.

This man's question was provocative. Assuming that I still have 10 per cent of life remaining, that is not much time. Now I am diligently praying about 7.6 more years in this world to use to His honor and glory. I rejoice each day as God allows me to continue to publish and communicate the Good News of the Gospel of Jesus Christ (Ps.96). I can't think of a more fulfilling way to spend this precious time on earth.

Some of the faithful servants of God mentioned above are contemporaries in the 40-100+ age group. For many of them, their most productive years were or are the latter years of their lives. God's grace in their lives has been evident *as they age to perfection* in the love, joy, and peace of the Lord.

Think with me also of the multiplied millions of Christian prayer warriors/bible students 40- 100+ who have never received any worldly acclaim but whose names are recorded in heaven. I delight in Paul's exhortation to the Galatians, "My little children, for whom I labor in birth again, until Christ is formed in you" (Gal.4:19). Christ-centered personality development[1]—being like Jesus—takes time. I thank God as I slowly age with agape love for Him.

Many of us like Paul have taught scripture over the years and have had labor pains for the students and ourselves. These labor pains continue until we see evidence of Christ being formed in our own lives and in the students. My prayer over the years has been "to grow in grace and in the knowledge of our Lord and Savior Jesus Christ" (2Pet.3:18). With the love, joy, and peace of the Lord to motivate us through His Holy Spirit at 40+ we are not "over the hill" but have just begun to climb to discover and enjoy with age our potential in Jesus Christ.

Since you became alive again, so to speak, when Christ arose from the dead, now set your sights on the rich treasures and joys of heaven where He sits beside God in the place of honor and power. Let heaven fill your thoughts, don't spend your time worrying about things down here. You should have as little desire for this world as a dead person does. Your real life is in heaven with Christ and God. And when Christ who is our real life comes back

---

[1]   Christ-Centered Personality Development, Dr. Robert Abarno, ©1988, Second Edition 1992, Third Edition 1994, Fourth Edition 1996. All rights reserved.

again, you will shine with Him and share in all His glories.

Away then with sinful, earthly things, deaden the evil desires lurking within you, have nothing to do with sexual sin, impurity, lust and shameful desires; don't worship the good things of life, for that is idolatry. God's terrible anger is upon those who do such things. You used to do them when your life was still part of this world; but now is the time to cast off and throw away all these rotten garments of anger, hatred, cursing, and dirty language.

Don't tell lies to each other; it was your old life with all its wickedness that did that sort of thing; now it is dead and gone. You are living a brand new kind of life that is contin- ually learning more and more of what is right, and trying constantly to be more and more like Christ who created this new life within you. In this new life one's nationality or race or education or social position is unimportant; such things mean nothing. Whether a person has Christ is what matters, and Christ is equally available to all.

Since you have been chosen by God who has given you this new kind of life, and because of His deep love and con- cern for you, you should practice tenderhearted mercy and kindness to others. Don't worry about making a good impression on them but be ready to suffer quietly and patiently. Be gentle and ready to forgive, never hold grudges. Remember, the Lord forgave you, so you must forgive others. Most of all, let love guide your life, for then the whole church will stay together in perfect harmony. Let the peace of heart which comes from Christ be always pre- sent in your hearts and lives, for this is your responsibility and privilege as members of His body. And always be thankful.

Remember what Christ taught and let His words enrich your lives and make you wise; teach them to each other and sing them out in psalms and hymns and spiritual songs, singing to the Lord with thankful hearts. And what-

ever you do or say, let it be as a representative of the Lord Jesus, and come with Him into the presence of God the Father to give Him your thanks.

COLOSSIANS 3:1-17

Praise God from whom all blessings flow for all time and eternity! Life in Christ has only just begun!

I can do all things through Christ who strengthens me.

PHILIPPIANS 4:13

My personal application and accountability with regard to Phillipians 4:13 is for me to continue to publish the "Good News of the Gospel of Jesus Christ." Application and accountability for my faith also includes physical conditioning (training for and running in the National Senior Olympics in 2001). Biblically for me this is related to running before a great cloud of witnesses (Heb. 12).

By God's grace I was enabled to compete in the 1989 and 1991 Senior Olympics. But in 1992 torn ligaments in my left foot disrupted my training for several years. At 76 I am just beginning to run again. I pray that by 2001 I will be able to qualify in the regional and state races to enable me to run in the nationals.

In addition to running the 1500-meter track event I would like to qualify for the 50-meter freestyle swimming event. If, by God's grace, I am able to compete my life will be enriched. Like Paul, I enjoy running the race God has set before me. However, spiritual endurance is my most Important race.

We also, since we are surrounded by so great a cloud of witnesses, let us lay aside every weight (aging), and the sin which so easily ensnares us, (at 40+) and let us run with endurance the race that is set before us. (Matt.28:19,20; Acts 1:8) looking unto Jesus, the author and finisher of our faith, who for the joy that was set before Him endured the cross, despising the shame, and has sat down at the right hand of the throne of God. For consider Him who endured

*such hostility from sinners against Himself, lest you become
weary and discouraged in your souls.*

H E B R E W S   1 2 : 1 - 3   (N K J V)

Running and swimming also condition my body, mind, and
spirit to pursue publishing the Good News about Jesus (Ps.96).
By God's grace the anticipation of writing, publishing, teaching,
advising, and counseling over the next seven+ years in concert
with my wife, family, and colleagues gives me purpose and
much joy. As these years begin to unfold I look forward with
keen anticipation to how God will use me as I live in the love,
joy, and peace of the Lord to His honor and glory.

*Eye has not seen, nor ear heard, nor have entered into the
heart of man, the things which God has prepared for those
who love Him.*

1   C O R I N T H I A N S   2 : 9

There are many 75+ saints I have observed in their daily
lives who are living in the love, joy, and peace of the Lord. A
few examples are:

A 90+ year old Christian lady who loves the Lord so much
that she shines with His love. Anyone who comes in contact
with Mrs. B cannot deny the glory which radiates from her face.
Despite the death of her husband she is very active with her
family, her church, and her girlfriends.

Mrs. B recently gave up driving her car because it required
so much attention to maintain even though according to Mrs. B
it was only a 1967 model. Her car has worn out but she has
not. Her mind, will, and emotions are intact. She is very perceptive and has good recent and remote memory. Her neighbors
are delighted with her personality which is definitely Christ-centered.

By any biblical measure she is holy and reflects the glory
of Jesus (Mrs. B is His reputation here on earth). The summit of
her faith is distinguished by His holiness. Mrs. B appears to be

able to do all things through Christ who strengthens her. Being in her presence brings one pure refreshment of soul. Her white hair is a halo and a crown of glory. One stands in awe as she speaks with such enthusiasm about the Lord and her life in Him.

There is another saint of God who at 77 volunteered as the caretaker and carpenter for his church. This Christian man retired 12 years ago but has remained active in service to the Lord. George also plays golf with his buddies, has a daily walking routine with his wife, and is available to anyone can use his considerable skills as a carpenter and as a prayer warrior. He has also taken on support of two children whose family is in desperate financial straits. He is a carpenter God is using to help build these young children into vessels for His service.

Despite the onset of cancer several years ago (which is now in remission praise God) George cannot remain inactive. He fixes things in the church almost before they are broken. George has built beautiful furniture for his wife and for the church. He is always available to help others and does so with great dignity.

Eye has not seen, nor ear heard, nor have entered into the heart of man, the things which God has prepared for those who love Him.

His quiet godly manner, his Christ-like dignity, and composure speak volumes about the summit of his faith. When you speak with him or spend time in his presence you see a man at 77 who is at "peace which is his position and practice of liberty in Christ." George has imperceptible amplitude...Jesus shines through him.

Another Biblical saint was John "the disciple who Jesus loved." John was a son of thunder, a rebellious young person who became a transitional man when He met Jesus. He followed the Lord for three years. John laid his head upon Jesus' chest in front of the other disciples unashamedly. The Lord received John's gesture of love, submission, and security. No one mocked or misunderstood the significance of John resting in Jesus, being strengthened for the work God had equipped him to do.

Later, through the power of the Holy Spirit, John wrote the Gospel of John, the epistles of John, and the Revelation of Jesus Christ. These writings have never been equaled in all of literature. This relatively unknown and unlearned man wrote with clarity, beauty, and power about the Lord and His Kingdom. John was unconcerned about aging (he was 90 when he wrote The Revelation of Jesus Christ) or about his exile. He was privileged to write The Revelation and then to return to Antioch to witness for His Lord and Savior.

John at the summit of his faith clearly perceived Jesus' holiness. He was enabled by God's grace through the leading of the Holy Spirit to record Jesus' high priestly prayer in John 17. Reading that chapter is a summit experience for the reader, an opportunity to ingest Jesus' holiness, the central theme of our Christ-centered lives. God's grace also enabled John to sum up the whole Bible in one verse (John 3:16):

> For God so loved the world that He gave His only begotten Son that whosoever believeth in Him should not perish but have eternal life.

As Christians are persecuted in this contemporary humanistic world, the authorities who exiled John similarly thought they were doing something to impede the message of God. Little did they realize that during his exile John was provided with an environment which allowed him to be disciplined and diligent to pursue the task God had blessed him with. Many of us feel that God has allowed us to be in a place and time that is not what we would have selected for ourselves. I contend that aging in this ungodly world is the best time and place to serve the Lord, die to self to live abundantly in Jesus with love, joy, and peace!

God protects and shields us with age to enable us to take

time for him and be productive in ways we would not choose for ourselves. We often do not recognize God's hand in our lives as we age. We are focused consciously and unconsciously on the negative facets of aging—aches and pains, inability to be as mobile as we used to be, have less energy, feel less productive, believe we are less relevant to others, etc. It does not seem to occur to many of my Christian brothers and sisters that age brings more, not less, opportunities to serve the Lord. We are so much better equipped than ever before. God knows this! He is ready to use us if we are willing to step up to our potential in Jesus (Eph. 1:3-12) and use our age and experience to His Glory!

I have a brother in Christ who is 65 and is experiencing a great amount of stress. He has been in the ministry 40 years and by the world's standards should retire.

However, he has been given a message from God for the whole body of Christ, the church. He is determined to be faithful and run the race God has set before him. I observe that his wife and he are moving together in peace to enable him to write and teach God's message. Everything in his being cries out to do God's will for his life!

This 65 year old brother I have referred to is living in the love, joy, and peace of the Lord which enables him to wage the battle to do God's will as a Christian soldier. He has confidence in his Lord Jesus that Satan will not prevail against him as he teaches the biblical message which God has given him. His enthusiasm for sharing this message is that of a man 25-30, not 65. We envision with peace that it may take another five years before he completes his biblical message under the direction of the Holy Spirit. He sees this time of prayer, study, and research as a gift from God.

Joshua was the man of God who led the Israelites into the promised land. God had taken Moses to be with Him and upon Joshua fell the mantle of Moses. Joshua's obedience to God by leading the Israelites into the possession of the land God had prepared for them was a prefigure of Jesus leading us into our promised land in heaven in the glorious presence of His Father. Joshua's name—Yeshua (Yahweh Is Salvation)—is the Hebrew equivalent of the name Jesus.

Joshua obeyed God in conquering Jericho by a method which appeared to others to be total foolishness. But God's wisdom always seems to be absolute foolishness to the world. Yet, when we obey God we are always victorious despite what the world considers to be "Christian religiosity ."

This Book of the Law shall not depart from your mouth, but you shall meditate in it day and night, that you may observe to do according to all that is written in it. For then you will have good success.

JOSHUA 1:8

Israel obeyed the Lord throughout the lifetimes of Joshua and the other old men who had personally witnessed the amazing deeds which the Lord had done for Israel.

JOSHUA 24:31 TLB

After Joshua had completed all that God has called him to do he went to be with the Lord at 110. What a great life Joshua had in service to the Lord God Almighty (1Cor.2:9). Joshua applied his faith and was accountable to His Creator.

Each of us can do all things through Christ who strengthens us! Saints in Christ 40-100+ continue to answer the question Francis Schaeffer asked, "How should we then live?"

Application of and accountability for our faith in Jesus is a joyful, exhilarating life experience.

Francis Schaeffer's video tape series in the 1970s pointed out that secular humanists and the elitists of academia, science, and government have attempted to fill the void in our world, but not with God. Schaeffer warned us that no civilization can exist or has ever existed without the absolute authority of Almighty God. Despite the fact that many cultures and civilizations have attempted to be successful without God, none have succeeded!

What then are we to do? The Bible calls us to holiness—the summit of our faith,

> *Just as He chose us in Him before the foundation of the world, that we should be holy and without blame before Him in love, to the praise of the glory of His grace, by which He has made us accepted in the Beloved.*

> EPHESIANS 1:4-6

Are those of us 40+ who are holy and act as His glory (His reputation here on earth) living examples of His love and grace? Isn't it exciting that we have this opportunity to be active and proclaim by our lives the love, joy, and peace of the Lord? Do we feel privileged to proclaim His love and grace with power from on high as we age in productive service to Him? Application of and accountability for our faith in Jesus is a joyful, exhilarating life experience.

In Jesus Christ hope springs eternal! The older we are in Jesus, the more useful we become. We are victorious survivors in Him!

Politicians and the mass media have tried to block the good news that Jesus saves. The print media and television media are committed to ungodly humanism and deliberately wage war on Christians. The Word of God is also derided within the liberal "church" and the humanistic world as symbolism and myth. Yet there has never been a better time in history for Christians to rejoice, pray without ceasing, give thanks, and step up in the strength and power of the Lord (Eph.6:10).

In Jesus Christ hope springs eternal! The older we are in Jesus, the more useful we become. We are victorious survivors in Him! There are countless examples of productive lives lived for Him despite age. The summit of our faith is His holiness which brings glory to His name. Enjoy the love and peace of the Lord, the best is yet to come. Let us give expression with the psalmist to the cry of our hearts:

> *Save me, O God, because I have come to you for refuge. I*
> *said to Him, You are my Lord, I have no other help but*
> *yours. I want the company of godly men and women in*
> *the land, they are the true nobility. Those choosing other*
> *gods shall all be filled with sorrow. I will not offer the sacri-*
> *fices they do or even speak the names of their gods. The*
> *Lord Himself is my inheritance, my prize. He is my food and*
> *drink, my highest joy! He guards all that is mine. He sees*
> *that I am given pleasant brooks and meadows as my*
> *share! What a wonderful inheritance! I will bless the Lord*
> *who counsels me, He gives me wisdom in the night. He*
> *tells me what to do. I am always thinking of the Lord, and*
> *because He is so near, I never need to stumble or fall.*
> *Heart, body and soul are filled with joy. For you will not*
> *leave me among the dead; you will not allow Your beloved*
> *one to rot in the grave. You have let me experience the*
> *joys of life and the exquisite pleasures of Your own eternal*
> *presence.*
>
> *PSALM 16 TLB*

Do you believe in dying to live abundantly at 40, 50, 60, 70, 80, 90, 100+ in the love, joy, and peace of the Lord? There is peace that passes all understanding as I age, die to self and the world and live abundantly here and now and for eternity.

God is ageless. Our eternal life in Jesus is similarly ageless. Eternal abundant life has just begun (John 10:10b).

God is ageless. Our eternal life in Jesus is similarly ageless.

I have enjoyed writing this book over the past four years. It was an experience in which God has allowed me to share with you some of the things he has taught me as I age with great enthusiasm. It is my privilege to have biblical intimacy with God who is my daily source of joy and delight. Everyday I see glimpses of His majesty, power and dominion, those manifestations of God which I expect from Him as King. But the reality of biblical intimacy with which He loves me is something that takes aging to fully receive and appreciate. I would not change anything in the process

Will you join me in Him?

of sanctification (crucifixion and resurrection) which I experience here and now with God. I live in Jesus abundantly now and know I will continue to enjoy His love and grace for eternity. Will you join me in Him?

Biblical Encouragement 40+

Eye has not seen, nor ear heard, nor have entered into the heart of man the things which God has prepared for those who love Him.

1 CORINTHIANS 2:9 NKJV

But the Godly shall flourish like palm trees, and grow tall as the cedars of Lebanon. For they are transported into the Lord's own garden, and are under His personal care. Even in old age they will still produce fruit and be vital and green. This honors the Lord, and exhibits his faithful care. He is my shelter. There is nothing but goodness in Him!

PSALM 92:12-14 TLB

For I have come here from heaven to do the will of God who sent me, not to have my own way. And this is the will of God, that I should not love even one of those He has given Me, but that I should raise them to eternal life at the Last Day. For it is my Father's will that everyone who sees His Son and believes on Him should have eternal life—that I should raise him at the Last Day.

JOHN 6:38-40 TLB

I can tell you this directly from the Lord: that we who are still living when the Lord returns will not rise to meet Him ahead of those who are in their graves. For the Lord Himself will come down from heaven with a mighty shout and with the soul-stirring cry of the archangel and the great trumpet-call of God. And the believers who are dead will be the first to rise to meet the Lord. Then we who are still alive and remain on earth will be caught up with them in the clouds to meet the Lord in the air and remain with Him forever. So comfort and encourage each other with this news.

1 THESSALONIANS 4:15-18 TLB

I prayerfully suggest that you make a list of things which God will enable you to accomplish for His Glory at 40-100+. Self-discovery, application, and accountability of who you are in Jesus and why you are here in Jesus comes through the study of His Word as you yield in obedience to His Holy Spirit.

God will reveal Himself to you as you yield in obedience to Him (John 14:21, 23). As Î age with the love, joy, and peace of the Lord I am excited each day as I pray and meditate on how I fit into His plan for my life.

God continues to reveal Himself to me more each day as I read and study His Word. Instead of reading a single passage or paragraph in my daily devotions; or to complete some assign-ment, or haphazardly read scripture, I now willingly and joyfully devote myself to know Him (2Pet.3:18). God knows my heart, my mind, my will and my emotions. I read His Word and listen carefully to the Holy Spirit as each word becomes my reality. My willing devotion is to pray and study scripture so that I can live for Him abundantly.

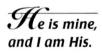
He is mine, and I am His.

God is allowing me to see each day the picture of my life that He has drawn in His Word. I am beginning to see clearly His purpose for my life. He is mine, and I am His not by chance but by His plan (Eph.3:1-12). Praise God!

His personal message to me about my life in Jesus is very specific. I know that I am and will continue to be a love letter from Him to a sick and dying world. What still amazes me though is that God uses me to help spread the Good News (Ps.96). Also that at 76 (and counting), God enables me to con-tinue to communicate that to know God is life eternal!

"And this is life eternal, that they might know thee, the only true God, and Jesus Christ, whom thou hast sent.

JOHN 17:3

Thank you, dear Lord Jesus. I stand in awe of You!

I invite you to join me in dying (our ongoing crucifixion) to live abundantly (our resurrection) here and now by living in the love, joy, and peace of the Lord at 40-100+. Eternal life has only just begun! **Enjoy Him; who you are in Him, why you are here in Him, and where you are going in Him!**

$\mathcal{S}$OLI DEO GLORIA!

$\mathcal{T}$O GOD ALONE
BE THE GLORY!

Afterthoughts

These afterthoughts have to do with completing a book which may or may not be read. That is of little consequence.

Not until these past few years have I had the opportunity to listen in depth to others who are peers, associates or teachers I respect. Most of my life had been spent in college, university and career in receiving information. I would have given much to have been educated in a tutorial system. No place to run. No place to hide. Dialogue in tutorials is the norm, inevitable and consequential. What is going on here and now at 76 is an ongoing tutorial with Jesus. Bob Mumford calls this "The Journey to Biblical Intimacy."[1]

Dying to Live Abundantly may have lost some of it's essence, not in wisdom from the Holy Spirit but because of me as the communicator of that wisdom. In retrospect, I wrote in didactic conformity, thereby limiting the freedom of my observations and experiences. I was unable therefore to fully share my vision of aging, crucifixion and resurrection. The environment of conformity in which I developed constrained me in method and content.

Growing up in the 1920's I was expected to conform. In my home, later in school, in the Marines, in business and in graduate school conformity to rote was the norm.

At 32 (in 1952) when I came to Jesus, I began to see a glimmer of hope, a break from conformity to biblical freedom. Writing this book in my 70's, despite it's inadequacies is a new beginning i.e., "The Truth shall make you free;" "You shall be free indeed" (John 8:32,36). The freedom I have in Jesus at 76, in biblical intimacy with the Father, is now being developed. I encourage others who are 40+ to engage Jesus; become bibli-

---

[1] The Journey to Biblical Intimacy, © Bob Mumford Library Series, Raleigh, NC 1996.

cally intimate with Him by giving expression of agape love in your life in service to Him. Your lives will become His glory, His reputation here on earth.

In Dr. Rolland Hein's biography of George MacDonald (StarSong, Nashville 1993), there is an illustration of an engraving William Blake created of an aged man entering the cave of death while from above the cave springs the resurrected body of the old man, now full of life and strength. Blake has captured in this engraving the freedom in Jesus from conformity to the old man worldly image of aging, dying and death.

Freedom in Jesus enables me to share with 40+ Christians a new beginning which I know will continue in intimacy with Jesus for eternity.